Choral Connections

LEVEL 4
MIXED VOICES

GLENCOE
McGraw-Hill

New York, New York
Columbus, Ohio
Mission Hills, California
Peoria, Illinois

Cover Photo: Peter Samuels Photography

Glencoe/McGraw-Hill

A Division of The **McGraw·Hill** *Companies*

Send all inquiries to:
Glencoe/McGraw Hill
15319 Chatsworth Street
Mission Hills, California 91345

ISBN 0-02-655535-2 (Student's Edition)
ISBN 0-02-655561-1 (Teacher's Wraparound Edition)

Printed in the United States of America.

2 3 4 5 6 7 8 9   MAL   02 01 00 99 98 97

Meet the Authors

Senior Author

Mollie G. Tower—As Coordinator of Choral and General Music of the Austin Independent School District, Mollie Tower was recently nominated as "Administrator of the Year." She is very active in international, national, regional, and state music educators' organizations. Ms. Tower was contributing author, consultant, and reviewer for the elementary programs *Share the Music* and *Music and You*. Senior author of *Música para todos, Primary and Intermediate Dual Language Handbooks for Music Teachers*, she has also written and consulted for many other publications. A longtime advocate of music education, Mollie is a popular clinician who conducts workshops across the country.

Milton Pullen
Professor of Music and Director of Choirs
After attending Texas A & I University where he acquired a Bachelor of Music Education in voice, Milton Pullen attended the University of Houston, where in 1976 he received a Master of Music in conducting. He has taught at the middle and high school levels for 24 years and for the last seven years has taught at the university level. He is now Professor of Music and Director of Choirs at Pepperdine University in Malibu, California.

Ken Steele
Director of Choral Activities
Ken Steele has taught secondary choral music for twenty-two years, having directed choirs at the middle school and high school levels. He received the Bachelor of Music degree from Stetson University in DeLand, Florida, and went on to the University of Texas in Austin to earn the Master of Music in Choral Literature and Conducting in 1971, studying with Dr. Morris J. Beachy. A member of Texas Music Educators Association, Texas Choral Directors Association, Texas Music Adjudicators Association, and a lifetime member of the American Choral Directors Association, he is currently the director of choral activities at L. C. Anderson High School, in Austin, Texas.

Gloria J. Stephens
Director of Choral Activities
With 23 years of teaching experience, Gloria Stephens is presently the Director of Choral Activities at Ryan High School in Denton, Texas. Mrs. Stephens earned her Bachelor of Music Education and Master of Music Education degrees from the University of North Texas in Denton. She has also done post-graduate work at Texas Woman's University in Denton, the University of Texas at Arlington, and Westminster Choir college in Princeton, New Jersey.

Consulting Author

Dr. Susan Snyder has taught all levels of vocal music over the last 25 years. She holds a B.S. in music education from the University of Connecticut and an M.A. from Montclair State College. She holds a Ph.D. in curriculum and instruction from the University of Connecticut and advanced professional certificates from Memphis State University and the University of Minnesota. Teaching at Hunter College and City University of New York, Dr. Snyder was coordinating author of the elementary music program, *Share the Music*, and a consultant on *Music and You*. She has published many articles on music education and integrated curriculum and is an active clinician, master teacher, and guest conductor.

Consultants

Choral Music
Stephan P. Barnicle
Choir Director
Simsbury High School
Simsbury, Connecticut

Vocal Development, Music Literacy
Katherine Saltzer Hickey, D.M.A.
University of California at Los Angeles
Los Angeles, California
Choir Director
Pacific Chorale Children's Choruses
Irvine, California

Music History
Dr. Kermit Peters
University of Nebraska at Omaha
College of Fine Arts
Department of Music
Omaha, Nebraska

Contributors/Teacher Reviewers

Dr. Anton Armstrong
Music Director and Conductor, St. Olaf Choir
St. Olaf College
Northfield, Minnesota

Jeanne Julseth-Heinrich
Choir Director
James Madison Middle School
Appleton, Wisconsin

Caroline Lyon
Ethnomusicologist
University of Texas at Austin
Austin, Texas

Caroline Minear
Supervisor
Orange County School District
Orlando, Florida

Judy Roberts
Choir Director
Central Junior High School
Moore, Oklahoma

Dr. A. Byron Smith
Choir Director
Lincoln High School
Tallahassee, Florida

Table of Contents

ADDITIONAL PERFORMANCE SELECTIONS

CHORAL MUSIC TERMS

Preparatory Material

Notes and Note Values

1 Whole Note

equals

2 Half Notes

equal

4 Quarter Notes

equal

8 Eighth Notes

equal

16 Sixteenth Notes

Rests and Rest Values

1 Whole Rest

equals

2 Half Rests

equal

4 Quarter Rests

equal

8 Eighth Rests

equal

16 Sixteenth Rests

Rhythm Challenge in 4/4 Meter

Directions: Accurately count and/or perform the following rhythms without stopping!

Rhythm Challenge in 6/8 Meter

Directions: Accurately count and/or perform the following rhythms without stopping!

Breathing Mechanics

Singing well requires good breath control. Support for singing comes from correct use of the breathing mechanism. Deep, controlled breathing is needed to sustain long phrases in one breath. Also, correct breathing will support higher, more difficult passages.

Posture
Posture is very important in breath support.
- Keep your body relaxed, but your backbone straight.
- To stretch your back: Bend over and slowly roll your back upward until you are standing straight again. Do this several times.
- Hold your rib cage high, but keep your shoulders low and relaxed.
- Facing front, keep your head level. Imagine you are suspended by a string attached to the very top of your head.
- When you stand, keep your knees relaxed, but do not "lock" them by pushing them all the way back. Keep your feet slightly apart.
- When you sit, keep both feet flat on the floor and sit forward on the edge of your chair.

Inhaling
- Expand the lungs out and down, pushing the diaphragm muscle down.
- Inhale silently without gasping or making any other noise.
- Keep the throat and neck muscles relaxed to maintain a feeling of space in the back of the mouth (picture a reverse megaphone).
- Imagine taking a cool sip of air through a straw, lifting the soft palate.
- Expand your entire waistline, keeping the chest high, and the shoulders relaxed, feeling the breath low in the body.

Breath Control
To help you develop breath control do the following:
- Hold one finger about six inches from your mouth imagining that your finger is a birthday candle. Now blow out a steady stream of air to blow out the flame of the candle.

Summary

STANDING
Feet slightly apart, one
slightly forward
Knees relaxed
Backbone straight
Rib cage high
Shoulders low
Head level

SITTING
Feet on the floor
Sit on edge of chair
Backbone straight
Rib cage high
Shoulders low
Head level

Solfège and Hand Signs

Solfège is a system designed to match notes on the staff with specific interval relationships. Hand signs provide additional reinforcement of the pitch relationships.

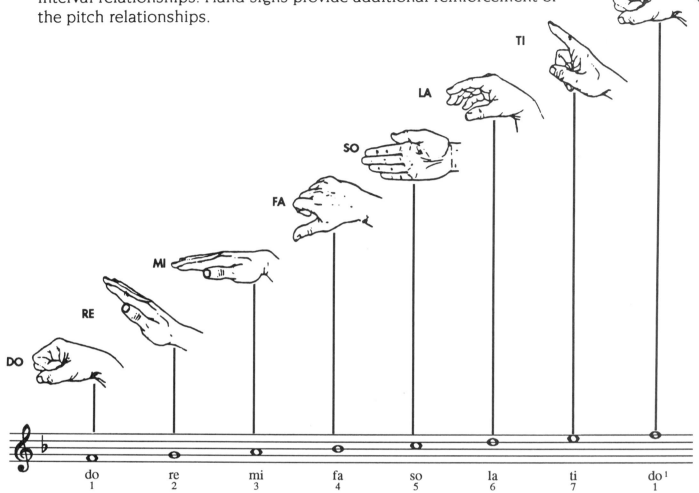

Frequently Found Intervals

An interval is the distance between two notes.

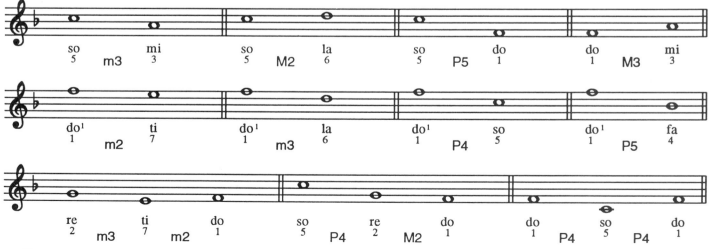

Pitch Challenge

Directions: Accurately sing each measure on solfège using hand signs and without stopping! During the measure of rest, look ahead to the next challenge.

Lessons

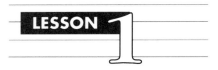

The One Who Stands Alone

COMPOSER: Joseph Martin
TEXT: J. Paul Williams and Joseph Martin

CHORAL MUSIC TERMS

4/4 meter

steady beat

style

3/4 meter

VOICING

SATB

PERFORMANCE STYLE

With reverence, power, and great expression
Accompanied by piano

FOCUS

- Explore styles of performing.
- Identify and perform with a steady beat.
- Conduct in 3/4 and 4/4 meter.

Warming Up

Vocal Warm-Up

Sing this exercise using *vah, veh, vee, voh,* or *voo.* Move up or down by half steps on the repeats. Sing the exercise using different styles, for example: light, heavy, marked, staccato, legato, and majestically (maestoso).

Sight-Singing

With a partner, point to one note at a time as your partner sings the correct pitch. Help each other until you feel the pitches naturally. Begin with stepwise intervals, then try larger intervals as confidence builds. Now switch roles so both of you get to practice.

Sight-sing this exercise using solfège and hand signs or numbers. Notice the meter changes. Conduct in 3/4 and 4/4 as you sing.

Singing: "The One Who Stands Alone"

The beat is not a sound, but a feeling.

You feel your heart beat, or the beat of a march. Beats are usually felt in sets. Here are the conducting patterns for beats in sets of 3 and 4. Practice these patterns so you can conduct "The One Who Stands Alone."

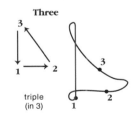
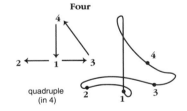

Now turn to the music for "The One Who Stands Alone" on page 4.

HOW DID YOU DO? ?	You've made a steady start with beats in sets of 3 and 4. Think about your preparation and performance of "The One Who Stands Alone." **1.** Describe how the beats are organized in "The One Who Stands Alone." **2.** Describe the style you used in "The One Who Stands Alone."	**3.** Sing the Sight-Singing exercise, conducting as you sing to show beats in sets of 3 and 4. **4.** Do you think the composer made good use of beat, meter, and style in "The One Who Stands Alone"? Support your opinion with facts from the piece.

The One Who Stands Alone

Music by Joseph M. Martin
Words by J. Paul Williams and
Joseph M. Martin

SATB, Accompanied

shout - ed from the moun - tains, "I have a dream,___ I have a

dream. I have a dream."___ Hear their voi - ces call like

thun - der down through time we hear their song. "Will you

give your - self for free - dom and be the

one who stands___ a - lone."

unis. **p**

There were some who served their na - tion who learned free - dom is-n't

out "I'll not sur - ren - der," "Give me li - ber-ty or give me

death... or give me death."___ Hear their voi - ces call like

thun - der down through time we hear their

thun - der   down through time   we hear   their

song.   "Will you   stand   and   face   the

63 *Triumphant to the end*

63 *Triumphant and building*

fu - ture,   will   you   stand   and   face   the

fu - ture, brave - ly stand and make a

fu - ture where no one

stands a - lone. Stands a - lone!

Siyahamba

South African Folk Song
ARRANGER: *Donald Moore*

CHORAL MUSIC TERMS

homophony
melodic leaps
register consistency
syncopated rhythm

VOICING

Three-part mixed

PERFORMANCE STYLE

Very rhythmic
Accompanied by piano with optional percussion

FOCUS

- Identify and perform syncopated rhythms.
- Sing melodic leaps with register consistency.
- Sing independently in three homophonic parts.

Warming Up

Rhythm Drill

Clap each of these rhythms, then combine them over an audible steady beat. Notice the syncopated rhythm that occurs when the emphasis is shifted off the beat.

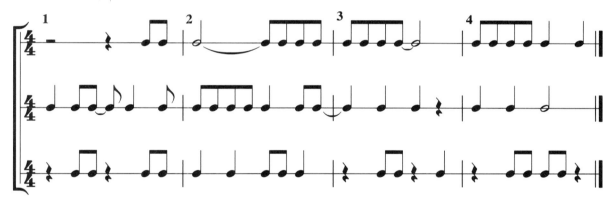

Vocal Warm-Up

Sing these scale passages on *nah*. Remember to use good breath support. Move up by half steps on the repeats. Keep the tone consistent from bottom to top and back again.

Sight-Singing

Sight-sing this exercise using solfège and hand signs or numbers. First sing each part separately, then put them together. Tune each chord carefully. Notice the syncopation and sing it crisply once the pitches are in place.

Singing: "Siyahamba"

In South Africa, there has been a long struggle for equality. "Siyahamba" is a Zulu song that has served as a call for freedom. "Siyahamba" provides a symbol of both unity and determination. Characteristic of Zulu vocal music, homophonic texture and syncopated rhythms have gained this style of music worldwide popularity. Perhaps you have heard this style of music before.

Now turn to the music for "Siyahamba" on page 15.

HOW DID YOU DO?

? ? ?

Unity and determination are Zulu ideals that work well in learning a new piece of music. Think about your preparation and performance of "Siyahamba."
1. How do you keep register consistency when you sing melodic leaps? Demonstrate by singing the first three pitches of "Siyahamba."
2. How well could you hold your part in tune when there were three parts sounding at once? Choose two classmates and demonstrate, using the Sight-Singing exercise.

3. Describe how syncopated rhythms are different from other rhythms. Point some out in "Siyahamba."
4. Explain the cultural background of "Siyahamba." How does knowing the cultural background of the piece change the way you prepare or perform it? If you were going to do an authentic performance of "Siyahamba," what would you need to know about the Zulu style that you don't already know?

Siyahamba

South African Folk Song
Arranged by Donald Moore (ASCAP)

Three-part Mixed, Accompanied with Optional Percussion*

*Percussion may be found on insert.

hamb' e - ku - kha - nye - ni kwen - kos. _____ Si - ya -

hamb' _____ e - ku - kha - nye - ni kwen - kos. _____ Si - ya -

hamb' e - ku - kha - nye - ni kwen - kos. _____ Si - ya -

*Use cue notes throughout only if range is a problem.

light of God. _ We are march-ing in the light of God. _ 1. We are

march - ing, _   march - ing, _ oh, _
30 ham - ba, _   ham - ba, _ oh, _

march - ing, _   march - ing, _   march - ing, _ oh, _   We are
ham - ba, _   ham - ba, _   ham - ba, _ oh, _   Si - ya -

1. 2. 3.   *

march - ing   in   the   light   of   God. _   *2. We are
hamb' e   ku - kha - nye - ni   kwen - kos. _   (Optional Words) 3. 4. Si - ya -

*Repeat as many times as desired

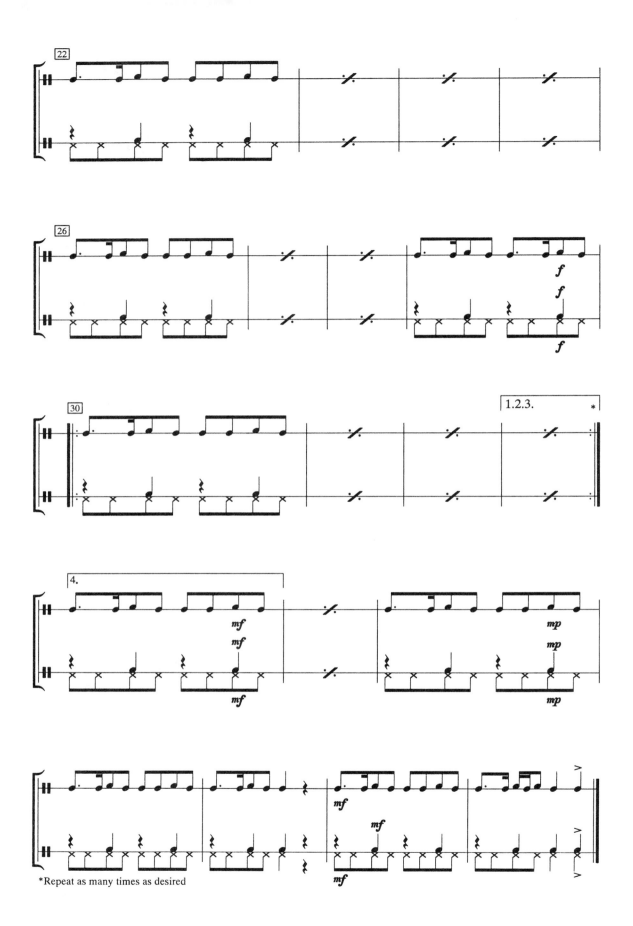

*Repeat as many times as desired

LESSON 3

The Prayer of Saint Francis

CHORAL MUSIC TERMS

legato articulation

phrasing

tuning

COMPOSER: *René Clausen*
TEXT: *St. Francis of Assisi*
(Giovanni Francesco Bernardone, 1182–1226)

VOICING

SATB

PERFORMANCE STYLE

Gently flowing
Accompanied by piano

FOCUS

* Recognize and sing using legato articulation.
* Identify out-of-tune singing, and tune pitches.
* Determine effective breathing technique to perform correct phrasing.

Warming Up

Vocal Warm-Up

Sing this exercise on *loo* using legato articulation. Move up a half step on each repeat. Vary the places where you breathe, for example: after each measure; after each two measures; after three measures; singing the last three on one breath. Now sing the whole phrase on one breath.

(Accompanist - Improvise arpeggios, rhythms, etc.)

Sight-Singing

Sight-sing this exercise using solfège and hand signs or numbers. Notice the sound of the full harmonies, and that each section moves against other parts, creating dissonances for resolution. Tune each pitch carefully. Use legato articulation, and breathe at the phrase markings.

Singing: *"The Prayer of Saint Francis"*

When composers begin with a text, they look for some meaning that can be enhanced by a musical setting. What type of text would you look for if you were a composer? Read aloud the text of "The Prayer of Saint Francis." What meaning does this text hold? Identify the negative and positive qualities related to peace mentioned in the text. Are they meaningful in the world today? How?

Now turn to the music for "The Prayer of Saint Francis" on page 25.

HOW DID YOU DO?

? ? ?

The composer set the text to music, and you have brought the combination of text and music to life with your performance. Think about your preparation and performance of "The Prayer of Saint Francis."

1. Describe legato articulation, and demonstrate it in the first phrase of "The Prayer of Saint Francis."

2. Can you tell whether pitches are in tune or not? Sing the Sight-Singing exercise in a quartet to demonstrate your ability to sing in tune.

3. How do you know where a phrase begins and ends? What does breathing have to do with phrasing? Demonstrate how you sing a phrase, using any phrase of "The Prayer of Saint Francis" you wish.

4. How did the composer enhance Saint Francis's ideas about qualities related to peace through music? Give specific examples, and describe the compositional devices and techniques used by the composer.

Commissioned by the Borger H.S. Varsity Choir, Johnny Miller, Director, for their performance at the Texas Music Educators Association Convention, February 6, 1992: Dedicated to his father, Bob Miller.

The Prayer of Saint Francis

By René Clausen

Starlight Lullaby

COMPOSER: *Philip Lane*
TEXT: *Peter Lawson*

CHORAL MUSIC TERMS

changing keys
half step
major tonalities
major scale
melody line
voice parts
whole step

VOICING

SATB

PERFORMANCE STYLE

Andante
Accompanied by piano

FOCUS

- Read and sing in major tonalities, changing keys.
- Identify characteristics of a major scale.
- Identify and sing melody lines that are shared between voice parts.

Warming Up

Vocal Warm-Up

Sing this exercise on *loo* using legato articulation on the quarter notes, and good diaphragmatic action to articulate the eighth notes. What other syllables might you use to sing this exercise? How do they feel different from *loo*?

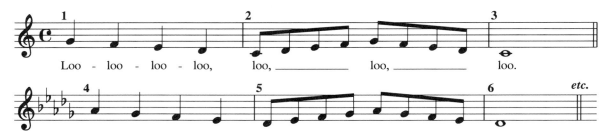

Sight-Singing

Sight-sing this exercise using solfège and hand signs or numbers. Count carefully as you sing. Notice the homophonic and polyphonic styles. Did you sing all the tones of the major scale? Does the same part have the melody throughout the exercise? Try sharing the melody between voice parts.

 Singing: "Starlight Lullaby"

A composer must make many choices. One is the tonal set to use. The major scale is a popular and comfortable tone set, made up of the following arrangement of steps:

whole   whole   half   whole   whole   whole   half

In C major, match these steps to the notes:

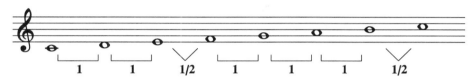

Other major scales have different pitches, but always the same arrangement of whole and half steps.

Now turn to the music for "Starlight Lullaby" on page 38.

Now turn to the music for "Starlight Lullaby" on page 38.

HOW DID YOU DO?

? ? ?

Each time you learn a new concept or skill, you take a step toward better musicianship. Think about your preparation and performance of "Starlight Lullaby."

1. Write a major scale and show the arrangement of whole and half steps.

2. How well can you sight-sing in major? If you were given a never-before-seen melody, what might be a problem for you?

3. Write a melody in C major, then give it to a classmate. Have the classmate read your melody by sight, and you read theirs. How well did you do? What could you do better?

4. When a melody line is shared between voice parts, what problems can occur? What can you do to solve these problems?

To Ian Tracey and the Royal Liverpool Philharmonic Choir

Starlight Lullaby

Philip Lane
Peter Lawson

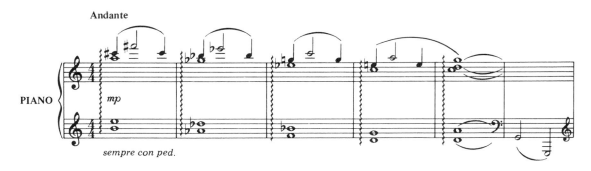

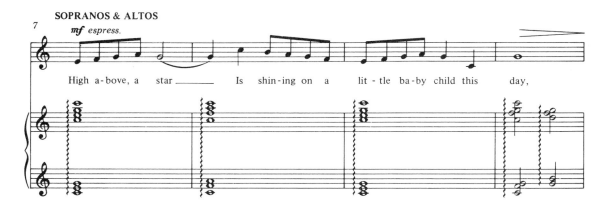

An orchestral version of the accompaniment is available for hire, scoring: 2.2.2.2 – 2.0.0.0 – hp. cel. str.

This piece is no. 2 of *Three Christmas Pictures*, a short choral and/or orchestral suite which may be performed separately or together. *Sleighbell Serenade* (no. 1) is also available separately (X357), and no. 3, *Christmas Eve Waltz*, is orchestral only.

© Oxford University Press 1993   Printed in Great Britain
OXFORD UNIVERSITY PRESS, MUSIC DEPARTMENT, WALTON STREET, OXFORD OX2 6DP

God Rest You Merry, Gentlemen

Traditional English Carol
ARRANGER: *James Neal Koudelka*

CHORAL MUSIC TERMS

augmentation

ensemble precision

half step

minor scale

minor tonality

round

whole step

VOICING

SATB

PERFORMANCE STYLE

Briskly
Accompanied by keyboard

FOCUS

- Identify and perform compositional devices of augmentation and round.
- Read and sing in minor tonality.
- Recognize characteristics of a minor scale.
- Sing in an ensemble with precision.

Warming Up

Rhythm Drill

Read and clap this rhythm with precision. Now divide into two groups. Half clap the rhythm as written, half clap it in augmentation, twice as slowly. Now clap it as a round, with Group 2 beginning four beats after Group 1.

Vocal Warm-Up

Sing this exercise slowly at first, tuning each note as you go. When the pattern is familiar, move up a half step on each repeat. Use different articulations and styles to keep it interesting, and challenge yourself.

Mi-hi, me-he, ma-ha, mo-ho, moo.

Sight-Singing

Sight-sing this exercise using solfège and hand signs or numbers. Notice the minor key, and sing accurately all *si's* (D#). This raised tone will feel like *ti* in a major key. Sing using both legato and staccato articulation, working for a precise ensemble sound. Once you know the exercise, sing with your eyes closed to hear the ensemble sound better.

Singing: "God Rest You Merry, Gentlemen"

Many traditional tunes are in minor tonality. There are three different kinds of minor scales: natural, harmonic, and melodic. The natural minor scale is made up of the following arrangement of steps:

whole   half whole   whole   half   whole   whole

In E minor, match these steps to the notes:

In minor, the tonal center is *la*. You use the pitch names of the relative major scale, in this case G major, to read the pitches in minor. In the harmonic minor, the seventh pitch is raised a half step. Instead of *so*, you will call it *si*.

Now turn to the music for "God Rest You Merry, Gentlemen" on page 47.

Now turn to the music for "God Rest You Merry, Gentlemen" on page 47.

HOW DID YOU DO?

Sometimes, pieces in minor can provide quite a challenge. Think about your preparation and performance of "God Rest You Merry, Gentlemen."

1. How precise is your singing? Sing the Sight-Reading exercise with three classmates to show your skill at singing with precision.
2. Write a minor scale and show the arrangement of whole and half steps.
3. How well can you sight-sing in minor?

If you were given a never-before-seen melody, what might be a problem for you?
4. Write a melody in E minor, then give it to a classmate. Have them read your melody by sight, and you read theirs. How well did you do? What could you do better?
5. Describe the compositional devices used by the arranger for each of the three verses of "God Rest You Merry, Gentlemen."

God Rest You Merry, Gentlemen

Traditional English Carol
Arranged by James Neal Koudelka

SATB Voices and Keyboard

save us all from Sa - tan's pow'r.   Com-fort and

which his moth-er Mar - y did noth-ing take in scorn; O ___ ti - dings of com-fort and

joy!   Joy!   Com - fort   and   joy!

joy, com-fort and joy, O ___ ti - dings of com - fort and joy!

(forcefully)

(slightly detached)
mp unis.

From

LESSON **6**

Papillon, Tu Es Volage

French Canadian Folk Song
ARRANGER: Jonathan Thompson

CHORAL MUSIC TERMS
lentemente
natural minor

VOICING
SATB

PERFORMANCE STYLE
Sweetly
A cappella

FOCUS
- Read and sing in natural minor.
- Sing using correct French pronunciation.

Warming Up

 Vocal Warm-Up
Sing this exercise using solfège and hand signs or numbers. Bounce on your toes as you sing, and keep your singing bouncy as well. What tonality is this exercise written in?

 Sight-Singing
Sight-sing this exercise using solfège and hand signs or numbers. Notice that all parts are written in the treble clef, but each may be sung in your vocal register. Choose any part you wish as you read and sing together. How would you describe these vocal parts in relationship to one another? Continue until you have sung all three parts.

Singing: "Papillon, Tu Es Volage"

Imagine a beautiful butterfly flitting from flower to flower. What might this butterfly symbolize in life? Read the text of "Papillon, Tu Es Volage" in English. What does the butterfly symbolize in this text?

Now turn to the music for "Papillon, Tu Es Volage" on page 56.

HOW DID YOU DO?

??????

When you learn a new piece, are you like a butterfly trying one thing and then another, or do you focus on one learning issue until it is mastered? Think about your preparation and performance of "Papillon, Tu Es Volage."
1. Describe how you read in natural minor, then sing either the Vocal Warm-Up or Sight-Singing exercise to demonstrate your ability.
2. Write a melody in a natural minor, then give it to a classmate. Have your classmate read your melody by sight, and you read theirs. How well did you do? What could you do better?

3. How is your French pronunciation? What is easy? What is difficult? Demonstrate your French pronunciation by reading aloud the first verse of "Papillon, Tu Es Volage."
4. Write a short essay describing the symbolism of the butterfly in "Papillon, Tu Es Volage."

Papillon, Tu Es Volage

Arranged by
Jonathan Thompson

SATB

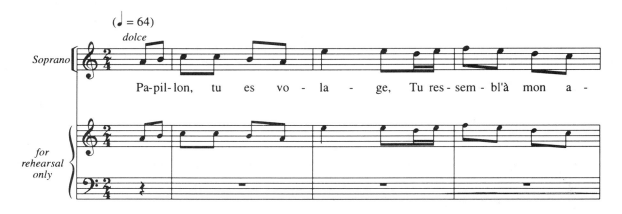

Papillon, tu es vo-la-ge, Tu res-sembl'à mon a-

mant. L'a-mour est un ba-di-na-ge, L'a-mour est un pas-se-

temps. Quand j'ai mon a-mant, J'ai le coeur con-tent!

Papillon, papillon, papillon,

Papillon, papillon, papillon,

Cro-yez-vous ma-de-moi-sel — le, Que je viens i-ci pour vous? J'en con-

Oh

Oh

nais d'au-tre plus bel — les, Qui ont les yeux bien plus doux. Soit dit en-tre

I Saw Three Ships

Traditional Carol
ARRANGER: *Edwin Fissinger*

VOICING

SATB

PERFORMANCE STYLE

Rocking, swaying
A cappella

FOCUS

- Identify, read, and clap in 6/8 meter.
- Distinguish between consonant and dissonant chords.
- Sing consonant and dissonant chords.

CHORAL MUSIC TERMS

consonant

dissonant

6/8 meter

Warming Up

Vocal Warm-Up

Stand and raise both hands over your head, then stretch upward. Lower your arms gradually, keeping them straight and extended. Sing this exercise using *koo*, keeping this posture to allow plenty of room for your breath. Move up by half steps on repeats, using legato articulation.

Sight-Singing

First clap the rhythm of each line to review 6/8 meter. Now sight-sing each line using solfège and hand signs or numbers. All four lines may be sung together. Try various ways to combine them.

Singing: "I Saw Three Ships"

What do you think is the difference between consonant and dissonant sounds? If all the bells on Earth rang at the same time, and you could hear them all, would the sound be consonant or dissonant? Listen to several sounds played together, and decide if the chord is consonant or dissonant. What intervals are more and less consonant to your ears?

Now turn to the music for "I Saw Three Ships" on page 64.

Now turn to the music for "I Saw Three Ships" on page 64.

HOW DID YOU DO?

If you worked together in harmony, you created dissonance in this piece. Think about your preparation and performance of "I Saw Three Ships."

1. You should be able to read and sing easily in 6/8 meter by now. How good are you at reading in this meter? Are there any patterns that you still find difficult? What can you do to improve?

2. Describe the difference between a consonant and dissonant chord, then demonstrate the difference in a small group.

3. Describe any dissonance in "I Saw Three Ships" and why these sounds are considered dissonant.

4. Write an essay describing the use of dissonant harmonies in "I Saw Three Ships," identifying where this occurs, and why the composer might have chosen this compositional device.

I Saw Three Ships

Traditional Carol
Arranged by Edwin Fissinger

SATB, A cappella

what was in those ships all three? On Christ-mas Day in the morn- ing. Our

what_ was in those ships all three? On Christ-mas Day in the morn- ing. Our

what was in those ships all three? On Christ-mas Day in the morn- ing.

what_ was in those ships all three? On Christ-mas Day in the morn- ing.

Sa- viour Christ and his la- dy, On Christ- mas Day, on Christ- mas Day, Our

Sa- viour Christ and his la- dy, On Christ- mas Day,_ on Christ- mas Day, Our

they sailed in- to Beth- le- hem, On Christ-mas Day in the morn- ing. And all the bells on

they sailed in- to Beth- le- hem, On Christ-mas Day in the morn- ing. And all the bells on

_(Day)_____ On Christ-mas Day in the morn- ing. And all the bells on

_(Day)_____ On Christ-mas Day in the morn- ing. And all the bells on

earth shall ring on Christ-mas Day, on Christ-mas Day, And all the bells on earth shall ring on

earth shall ring on Christ-mas Day, on Christ-mas Day, And all the bells on earth shall ring on

earth shall ring on Christ-mas Day, on Christ-mas Day, And all bells on earth shall ring on

earth shall ring on Christ-mas Day, on Christ-mas Day, And all bells on earth shall ring on

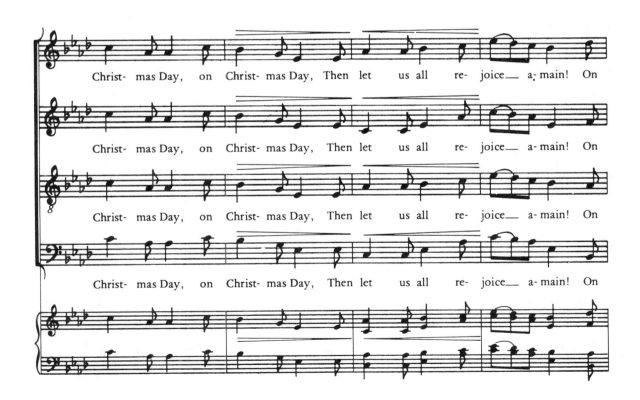

LESSON 8

African Noel

ARRANGER: *André J. Thomas*

CHORAL MUSIC TERMS

changing meter

constant beat

rhythm

sight-reading

2/4 meter

VOICING

Four-part chorus

PERFORMANCE STYLE

Rhythmically, joyously
A cappella with optional unpitched percussion

FOCUS

- Sight-read and sing focusing on rhythm.
- Conduct in 2/4 meter.
- Perform with a constant beat in changing meter.

Warming Up

Vocal Warm-Up

Sing this exercise using *doo* or whatever syllables come spontaneously to mind. The brisk motion and quick rhythms require clear articulation. While singing, roll the shoulders, shake out the arms, loosen the neck area, and do it rhythmically with the music. Move up and down by half steps on each repeat. Notice the tied note, and feel the syncopation as you sing.

doo doo doo . . .

Sight-Reading

Rhythm is one of the keys to sight-singing success. Make a plan before you begin reading, choose a tempo, and look ahead for upcoming problem spots. Really focus and do your best the first time through. After speaking and clapping this rhythm, sing it using pitches of your choice from the B♭ major tonic chord (B♭, D, F). Sing using different combinations of *doo-bee-doot*.

Singing: "African Noel"

Imagine that your first reading of a piece was evaluated.

Would your sight-reading skills be considered good? excellent?

To read well, you must be able to read rhythms. What "system" do you use for rhythmic reading? What other ways do you help yourself read rhythms well?

Now turn to the music for "African Noel" on page 73.

HOW DID YOU DO?

Good reading skills lead to good performance. Think about your preparation and performance of "African Noel."
1. Did your ability to sight-read rhythm improve during this lesson? How? How do you know?
2. Read and speak the Sight-Reading exercise, conducting in 2/4 meter.

3. The meter changes from 2/4 to 3/8 to 2/8 to 4/4 during "African Noel." Describe how these meter changes work, then clap the tenor line rhythm from measure 53 to the end to show your ability to perform changing meters.

For Anton Armstrong and the St. Olaf Choir

African Noel

Arranged by André J. Thomas

Four-part Chorus of Mixed Voices, A cappella

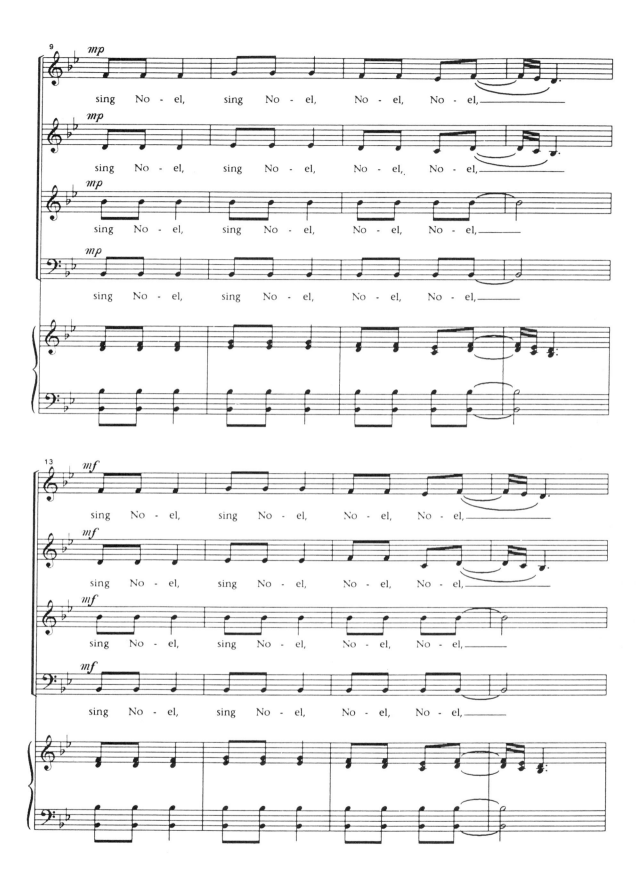

The Lord Is My Shepherd

Psalm 23, *paraphrased*

COMPOSER: *Allen Pote*

CHORAL MUSIC TERMS

major tonality

phrase

sight-sing

sixths

thirds

tuning

unison/octaves

upbeat entrance

VOICING

SATB

PERFORMANCE STYLE

Calmly
Accompanied by piano

FOCUS

- Identify and sing phrases using correct phrasing techniques.
- Prepare and breathe correctly for upbeat entrances.
- Sight-sing in major tonality.
- Tune unison/octaves, thirds, and sixths.

Warming Up

Rhythm Drill

First read and clap these rhythms. Then add the words. Feel each example as a complete phrase, with a beginning, peak, and ending. Notice which phrases have upbeat entrances, and decide how many beats you need for a full preparatory breath.

Vocal Warm-Up

Take a breath through the nostrils only, then sing this exercise on *ah*. Move up a half step on each repeat. Feel the soft palate rising as you breathe, and sing with a dropped jaw.

Sight-Singing

Sight-sing this exercise using solfège and hand signs or numbers. Identify each harmonic interval as a unison, octave, third, fourth, or sixth. Challenge yourself to read accurately the first time through, and be sure to tune as you sing.

Singing: "The Lord Is My Shepherd"

Can you sight-read rhythm and pitch at the same time? If you can, you're an excellent sight-reader! What strategies do you use when you sight-sing? What clues can help you be a successful reader?

Now turn to the music for "The Lord Is My Shepherd" on page 86.

HOW DID YOU DO?

?
?
?

Once you can read rhythm and pitch, you'll have plenty of time to work on phrasing and interpretation. Think about your preparation and performance of "The Lord Is My Shepherd."
1. What makes the phrases in "The Lord Is My Shepherd" unusual? How did you decide to shape the phrases? Was it successful?
2. Tell how the rests at the beginning of phrases affected your breath preparation for phrases. Sing a phrase with an upbeat entrance to demonstrate your ability.

3. Is your sight-singing ability improving? Describe your ability, and your progress.
4. Sing from measure 55–end of "The Lord Is My Shepherd" in a quartet, showing your ability to sing and tune unison/octaves and intervals.

For the San Francisco Bay Area Chapter of Choristers Guild
in celebration of their fifth Youth Choir Festival

The Lord Is My Shepherd

Psalm 23, paraphrase A.P.

Allen Pote

in fields of green, leads me be - side still

wa - ters.

The Lord is my shep - herd,

The Lord is my

Forest Cool, Thou Forest Quiet

CHORAL MUSIC TERMS

dynamics

independent singing

intensity

morendo

phrase

COMPOSER: *Johannes Brahms* (1833–1897)

EDITED BY: S. *Stephen Barlow*

VOICING

SATB

PERFORMANCE STYLE

Slowly and sweetly

A cappella

FOCUS

- Identify and sing phrases using intensity.
- Sing one part independently when four parts are being sung.
- Sing using correct German pronunciation.

Warming Up

Vocal Warm-Up

Conduct as you sing this warm-up using solfège and hand signs or numbers. Give special attention to the dynamics. Move up or down by half steps on repeats.

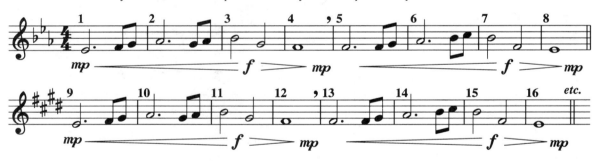

Sight-Singing

Sight-sing each voice line separately, first without dynamic intensity, then with it. Now sing in full ensemble, with dynamic intensity. Notice that "x" marks the beginning, peak, and release of each phrase.

Singing: "Forest Cool, Thou Forest Quiet"

Imagine that you are holding a soft-drink can that has been shaken. What is going on inside the can? What might happen if you open the can? What happens inside if you don't open it? Think of your breath as the carbonation or energy in the beverage. When the dynamics in a musical performance stir up the "carbonation," an intensification from the beginning of each phrase to the peak, and then release energy to the end of the phrase. Just like the energy inside the can, you must keep the intensity always under control as it is stirred up by the emotion of the music.

Now turn to the music for "Forest Cool, Thou Forest Quiet" on page 98.

HOW DID YOU DO?

This piece was really intense. Think about your preparation and performance of "Forest Cool, Thou Forest Quiet."

1. Describe how you shaped the phrases in "Forest Cool, Thou Forest Quiet." In a quartet, sing a phrase to demonstrate your ability to shape phrases with intensity.

2. Can you hold your part when three other parts are being sung? When is it most easy? When is it most difficult? Do a performance of measures 1–17 in a quartet, demonstrating your skill.

3. How good is your German pronunciation? Read a phrase or two to demonstrate.

4. Why do you suppose "Forest Cool, Thou Forest Quiet" is considered a great piece of music? Do you think it is great? Why or why not? Give specific examples from the piece to support your argument.

5. Do you personally like "Forest Cool, Thou Forest Quiet"? Why or why not?

Forest Cool, Thou Forest Quiet

Waldesnacht, du Wunderkühle

SATB Chorus

Johannes Brahms
Edited by S. Stephen Barlow
English Text by S.S.B.
(ASCAP)

LESSON 11

Keep Your Lamps!

Spiritual
ARRANGER: *André J. Thomas*

CHORAL MUSIC TERMS

accent

minor tonality

syncopation

VOICING

SATB

PERFORMANCE STYLE

Moderately
Accompanied by conga drums

FOCUS

- Identify and perform written accents.
- Identify and perform accents created by syncopation.
- Identify and sing in minor tonality.

Warming Up

Body Warm-Up

Do this stepping and clapping exercise until it becomes natural and familiar. Clap each line several times. The claps create a pattern of accents over the steady beat steps.

HANDS:	*Clap*		*Clap*	
FEET:	Step Left	Close Right	Step Left	Close Right

HANDS:		*Clap*		*Clap*
FEET:	Step Right	Close Left	Step Right	Close Left

HANDS:			*Clap*	
FEET:	Step Left	Close Right	Step Left	Close Right

HANDS:				*Clap*
FEET:	Step Right	Close Left	Step Right	Close Left

 Vocal Warm-Up

Sing this exercise with great energy on *doot*. Notice the minor and major triads as you sing, and tune the third carefully. Add accents to some pitches—decide before you sing. Move up by half steps on each repeat.

doot   doot . .

etc.

Sight-Singing

Sight-sing each line separately, reading rhythm and pitch together. Focus carefully for accuracy the first time through. Notice the accents marked with accent marks, and find the one created by syncopation. How will you combine these lines? Try different combinations until you have sung each line.

Singing: *"Keep Your Lamps!"*

An accent indicates a sound that has more stress than the sounds around it. There are two kinds of accents in music—those caused by more stress (>), and those caused by unexpected stress or duration (syncopation).

Read this sentence without any accents:

Jill is our best fan.

Now read it with the accents shown:

> >
Jill is our best fan.   Jill **is** our best fan.   Jill is **our** best fan.

> >
Jill is our **best** fan.   Jill is our best **fan**.

To create syncopation, stretch one of the syllables out longer, or say it off the beat.

Now turn to the music for "Keep Your Lamps!" on page 107.

Now turn to the music for "Keep Your Lamps!" on page 107.

HOW DID YOU DO?

? ?

"Keep Your Lamps!" will be an accent in your program. Think about your preparation and performance of "Keep Your Lamps!"
1. Describe how you recognize written accents, and what they tell you to do.
2. Describe syncopation and tell why it is considered an accent.
3. Sing the natural minor scale, then the harmonic minor scale. Tell which is used in

"Keep Your Lamps!" and then sing from measures 8–16 using solfège and hand signs or numbers to show your ability to sing in minor.
4. Describe the ensemble's performance of "Keep Your Lamps!" What was good, and what needs work?
5. Identify what you like about "Keep Your Lamps!" What would you change if you were writing the arrangement?

Keep Your Lamps!

Spiritual
Arranged by André J. Thomas

Mixed Voices, SATB, with Conga Drums

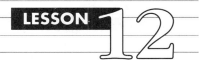

LESSON 12

Blessed Are the Pure of Heart

CHORAL MUSIC TERMS

homophonic

mental image of sound

polyphonic

Romantic period

vocal tone color

COMPOSER: *Woldemar Voullaire* (1825–1902)

EDITED BY: K. *Köpe*

TRANSLATOR: R. *Steelman*

VOICING

SATB

PERFORMANCE STYLE

Andante

Accompanied by organ

FOCUS

- Sing using vocal tone colors drawn from mental images of sound.
- Identify and perform a full, rich, Romantic period vocal sound.
- Sing polyphonic and homophonic textures.
- Sing with correct German pronunciation.

Warming Up

Vocal Warm-Up

Sing this warm-up employing the five basic vowels, preceded by a voiced consonant (*m* or *n*). Strive for a warm, full sonority. Conduct in 4/4 while repeating this exercise up or down by half steps. Notice that the parts move together, creating a homophonic texture.

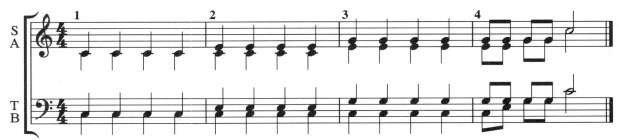

Sight-Singing

Sight-sing this exercise using solfège and hand signs or numbers, and a rich, warm tone color. Read each melody through, trying for accuracy the first time through. Then divide into three parts, each combining the melodies into a different pattern—1, 2, 3; 2, 3, 1; 3, 1, 2. Sing through all the melodies from where you begin. Which part is most difficult? Why?

Singing: "Blessed Are the Pure of Heart"

Your voice can reproduce any sound you can hear and any sound your brain can imagine. Make the sound of a small dog, then a medium dog, and finally a large dog.

Sing the Vocal Warm-Up in the following ways:

- a young child singing
- young teenagers singing
- seniors in high school singing
- adults singing

Your mind will tell your voice the tone quality it wants to use, then you will produce that sound.

What will your mind tell your voice to do to create a Romantic period vocal tone?

Now turn to the music for "Blessed Are the Pure of Heart" on page 113.

Now turn to the music for "Blessed Are the Pure of Heart" on page 113.

HOW DID YOU DO?

Using appropriate style is one key to excellent performance. Think about your preparation and performance of "Blessed Are the Pure of Heart."

1. Describe what the mind has to do with vocal tone color. Demonstrate with several different examples of tone colors you can imagine and sing.

2. Describe a Romantic period vocal sound, then demonstrate it using the first phrase of your voice part of "Blessed Are the Pure of Heart."

3. Describe and distinguish between polyphonic and homophonic textures, pointing them out in "Blessed Are the Pure of Heart."

4. How well did you pronounce the German in this piece? What made it easy? What was difficult?

5. Describe the ensemble's performance of "Blessed Are the Pure of Heart." What was good, and what needs work?

Blessed Are the Pure of Heart

(Selig Sind Die Reines Herzens Sind)

Mixed Voices, SATB, with Organ

Woldemar Voullaire (1825–1902)
Edited by K. Köpe
English by R. Steelman

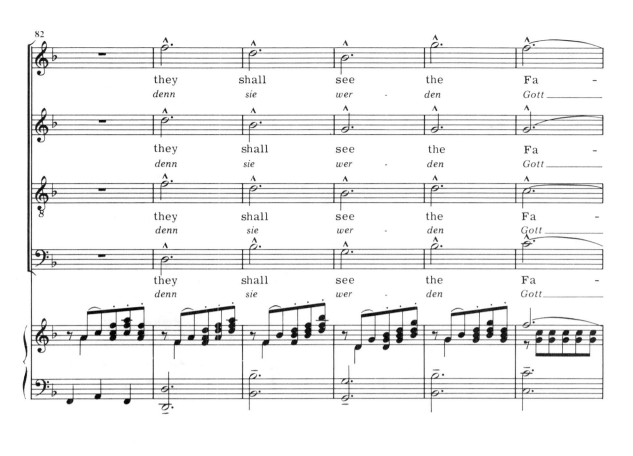

V'amo di Core

COMPOSER: *Wolfgang Amadeus Mozart (1756–1791)*

CHORAL MUSIC TERMS

canon

independent singing

Italian language

round

VOICING

SATB

PERFORMANCE STYLE

Procession
A cappella, for three four-part choruses

FOCUS

- Sing independently.
- Identify and sing in a round.
- Distinguish between round and canon.
- Sing with correct Italian pronunciation.

Warming Up

Vocal Warm-Up

Sing this warm-up using solfège and hand signs or numbers. Stand on part 1, sit on part 2, sit with crossed legs and arms on part 3. Sing this exercise as a three part canon, with the movements. Decide on a good place to end all together. Notice the pitches of the tonic chord.

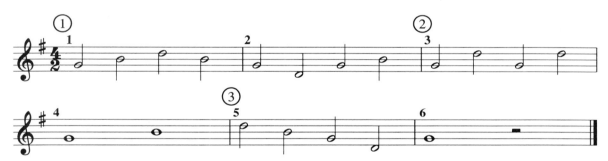

Sight-Singing

Sight-sing this exercise using solfège and hand signs or numbers. Can you sight-sing it with all four parts right away? Once the full ensemble is familiar with the piece, divide into three choirs of four parts, and sing the exercise as a canon. Decide on a good place to end all together.

Singing: "V'amo di Core"

In the "good old days" before television and radio, singing was a popular evening activity. Rounds were very popular because everyone could learn the same part together, then make complex-sounding music with comparative ease.

How would you describe a round? Do you know the difference between a round and a canon? (In a round all voice parts end separately; in a canon all voice parts end at the same time.) Rounds and canons can be very complex, if the composer is very clever. Sing a round as part of your warm-ups each day.

Now turn to the music for "V'amo di Core" on page 125.

HOW DID YOU DO?

? ? ?

Mozart was one of the most imaginative composers in history. Think about your preparation and performance of "V'amo di Core."

1. How well could you hold your part independently when the piece was sung in four parts? Did that change when your ensemble became three four-part choruses and sang in a round?

2. Describe a round and a canon, and identify the difference between them.
3. Sing the Vocal Warm-Up, or some other canon of your choice, with at least two other classmates—one person on a part.
4. How well did you pronounce the Italian in this piece? What language, other than English, do you find easiest to sing? Hardest?

V'amo di Core
Kanon für three vierstimmigre Chöre*

Wolfgang Amadeus Mozart

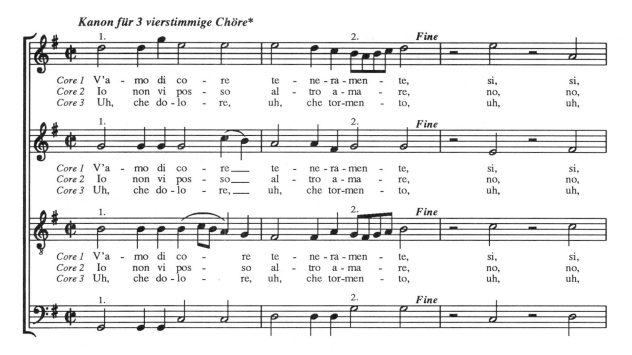

*) Die Chöre, deren jeder seinen eigenen Text singt, schlissen nacheinander beim Fine.–
Textunterlegung vom Herausgeber überarbeitet (vgl. Anm. S. 2 unten).

Chor 1 Zärt - lich von Her - zen muss ich dich lie - ben, ju, ja,
Chor 2 Kann nur dich lie - ben, nie von dir las - sen, nie, nie,
Chor 3 O, wel-cher Jam - mer, o, wel-che Qua - len, o, o,

Chor 1 Zärt - lich von Her - zen___ muss ich dich lie - ben, ju, ja,
Chor 2 Kann nur dich lie - ben,___ nie von dir las - sen, nie, nie,
Chor 3 O, wel-cher Jam - mer,___ o, wel-che Qua - len, o, o,

Chor 1 Zärt - lich von Her - zen muss ich dich lie - ben, ju, ja,
Chor 2 Kann nur dich lie - ben, nie von dir las - sen, nie, nie,
Chor 3 O, wel-cher Jam - mer, o, wel-che Qua - len, o, o,

Chor 1 Zärt - lich von Her - zen muss ich dich lie - ben, ju, ja,
Chor 2 Kann nur dich lie - ben, nie von dir las - sen, nie, nie,
Chor 3 O, wel-cher Jam - mer, o, wel-che Qua - len, o, o,

zärt-lich von Her - zen muss ich dich lie - ben, ja, ja!
kann nur dich lie - ben, nie von dir las - sen, nie, nie!
o, wel-cher Jam - mer, o, wel-che Qua - len, o, o!

zärt-lich von Her - zen muss ich dich lie - ben, ja!
kann nur dich lie - ben, nie von dir las - sen, nie!
o, wel-cher Jam - mer; o, wel-che Qua - len, o!

zärt - lich von Her - zen, ja, ja, ja!
nie___ von dir las - sen, nie, nie, nie!
o, ___ wel-cher Jam - mer, o, o, o!

zärt - lich von Herzen, ja, muss ich dich lie - ben, ja!
nie von dir lassen, nie, nie von dir las - sen, nie!
o, welcher Jammer, o, o, wel-che Qua - len, o!

(Deutsche Textübertragung: Gottfried Wolters)
Aus: Mozart Kanons im Urtext, herausgegeben von Gottfried Wolters, Finken - Bücherei, Bd.
1/2, Mössler Verlag, Wolfenbüttel. (Dort mit Anmerkungen und Revisions - Bericht).

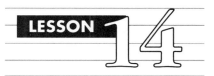
I Will Lay Me Down in Peace

COMPOSER: *Healey Willan*

CHORAL MUSIC TERMS

independent singing

melodic skips

melodic steps

rhythmic interplay

tone painting

VOICING

SATB

PERFORMANCE STYLE

Slow and soft

A cappella

FOCUS

- Read and sing independently parts with rhythmic interplay.
- Identify and sing melodic steps and skips accurately.
- Identify combination of text and music, or tone painting.

Warming Up

Vocal Warm-Ups

1. Sing this warm-up using *hoo*. Notice the articulation, and use good diaphragmatic action for clear articulation. Be sure to keep the third in tune as you sing. Move up by half steps on each repeat. Change the vowel after *h* (*ha, ho, hi, hee,* etc.) to keep this exercise interesting.

2. Sing this exercise using solfège and hand signs or numbers, then text. Then sing it in a three part round, at a moderate tempo. Listen to the harmonies that result from the combination of voices. Notice the steps and skips in the melody. Tenors and Basses, sing with a light tone in the upper register to match that of the Sopranos and Altos.

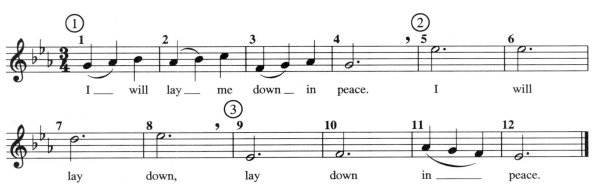

Sight-Singing

Sight-sing this exercise using solfège and hand signs or numbers. Tune carefully to the parts around you, and listen for the rhythmic interplay among the parts.

Singing: "I Will Lay Me Down in Peace"

A jigsaw puzzle is a combination that is greater than the sum of its parts because each of the pieces contributes to completing the whole picture. Text and music unite to create an expressive force. Read the text of "I Will Lay Me Down in Peace." Now sing or listen to each line separately, and describe the leaps and steps. How does each line enhance the text? How does the combination of melodies enhance the text? The composer has made a tone painting in which text and music express more than the text alone.

Now turn to the music for "I Will Lay Me Down in Peace" on page 129.

HOW DID YOU DO?

?
?
?

The combination of text and music is only as powerful as your performance. Think about your preparation and performance of "I Will Lay Me Down in Peace."
1. How well could you hold your part independently when the piece was sung in four parts? What is different about this piece than others you have sung lately?
2. Describe the rhythm of "I Will Lay Me Down in Peace" and explain how it adds to the meaning of the text. Give general and specific examples.

3. Describe the use of melodic steps and skips in "I Will Lay Me Down in Peace" and explain how it adds to the meaning of the text. Give general and specific examples.
4. Sing "I Will Lay Me Down in Peace" in a quartet to show your ability to hold your part, and sing the rhythms and pitches accurately.
5. Describe what it means when a composer tone paints a text. Give examples of when and how this occurs in "I Will Lay Me Down in Peace."

I Will Lay Me Down in Peace

Healey Willan

Quartet or Chorus

The Cloths of Heaven

COMPOSER: *Adolphus Hailstork*
TEXT: *William Butler Yeats* (1865–1939)

CHORAL MUSIC TERMS

altered tones

melodic leaps

staggered breathing

tuning pitches

VOICING

SATB

PERFORMANCE STYLE

With flexibility, slowly
A cappella

FOCUS

- Tune pitches accurately.
- Read and sing melodic leaps with accuracy.
- Read and sing altered tones using solfège and hand signs or numbers.
- Use staggered breathing.

Warming Up

Vocal Warm-Up

Are you ready for a challenge? This exercise is a serious study in tuning. Sing this warm-up on the text provided. Notice that with each new measure, one voice raises its pitch by a half step. On the fourth measure, the alto and bass move up together. Stagger your breathing so there are no breaks over a bar line. Listen carefully as you sing!

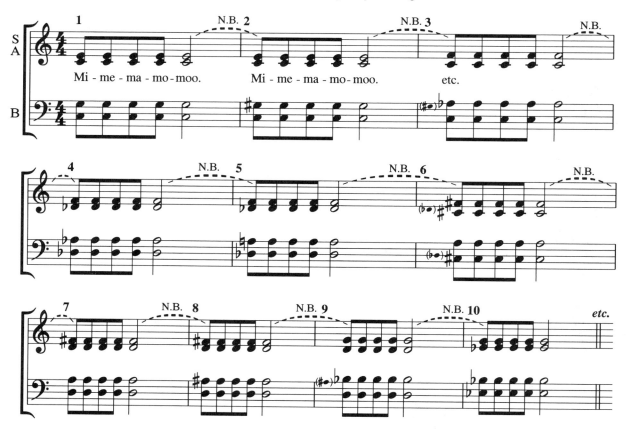

Sight-Singing

Here's another challenge for you! This exercise is written with many uncommon leaps and several altered tones. It will prepare you for the upcoming piece, so take the time to become familiar with the intervals and style. Can you perfect the melody so the pitches are exactly in tune when you sing each one?

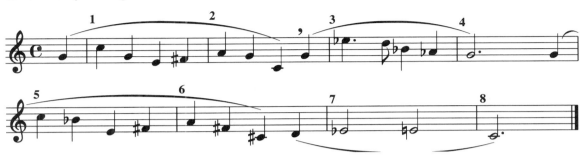

Singing: "The Cloths of Heaven"

If the richness and beauty of heaven were represented in an embroidered cloth, what do you imagine it would look like? Read the text of "The Cloths of Heaven," then explain the message in your own words.

> Had I the heavens' embroidered cloths,
> Enwrought with golden and silver light,
> The blue and the dim and the dark cloths
> Of night and light and the half-light.
> I would spread the cloths under your feet:
>
> But I, being poor, have only my dreams:
> I have spread my dreams under your feet,
> Tread softly because you tread on my dreams.
> —William Butler Yeats

If you were going to compose a setting to enhance this text, in twentieth-century style, what musical characteristics and compositional techniques might you use?

Now turn to the music for "The Cloths of Heaven" on page 134.

HOW DID YOU DO?

? ? ? ?

You have embroidered your own sound painting. Think about your preparation and performance of "The Cloths of Heaven."

1. Describe the challenge of singing in tune in "The Cloths of Heaven," then tell how well you did.

2. Choose a section of "The Cloths of Heaven" to sing with three classmates, demonstrating your ability to sing melodic leaps and altered tones, and to stagger your breathing.

3. Describe the musical characteristics and compositional techniques the composer used to tone paint the text. Was this treatment effective?

4. Did you predict the compositional techniques that the composer used? What else might you have suggested?

5. If you were going to give advice to an ensemble that was just beginning to learn this piece, what would you tell them in order to guide them to a really effective and convincing performance?

The Cloths of Heaven

No. 4 from *Five Short Choral Works*

Adolphus Hailstork
William Butler Yeats (1865–1939)

SATB, A cappella

Ave Maria

COMPOSER: *Franz Biebl*

CHORAL MUSIC TERMS
conductor
dissonant harmonies
Latin language
tuning pitches

VOICING

SATB

PERFORMANCE STYLE

Quietly flowing
A cappella

FOCUS

- Tune pitches accurately.
- Read and sing in dissonant harmonies accurately.
- Follow the conductor.
- Sing using correct Latin pronunciation.

Warming Up

Vocal Warm-Up

Sing this exercise using the text provided with a full rich sound and legato articulation. Watch and follow your conductor, who may decide to go faster or slower at any time!

Sight-Singing

Sight-sing these two examples using solfège and hand signs or numbers. Identify the musical characteristics of each, and tell if you think they come from the same piece or two different pieces, and what clues there are to support your theory.

Singing: "Ave Maria"

Imagine you are a conductor of a fine ensemble. They are preparing, with your guidance, to perform a piece that has two separate groups, both performing at the same time. Each group has different music, but the two parts fit together.

What problems might occur in this conducting situation? What might the conductor do to minimize this situation? What can the singers do to help?

Now turn to the music for "Ave Maria" on page 142.

HOW DID YOU DO?

? ? ?

You have embroidered your own sound painting. Think about your preparation and performance of "Ave Maria."
1. Describe the challenge of singing in tune in "Ave Maria," then tell how well you did.
2. Choose a section of "Ave Maria" which you found difficult to learn, and sing it showing how accurately you have learned the pitches.
3. Discuss the role of the conductor, and why it is especially important in the performance of "Ave Maria." What is the performer's responsibility regarding the conductor?

4. How well did you pronounce the text in Latin? What was easy? What needs work?
5. If you were going to conduct an ensemble in learning and performing this piece, how would you go about introducing it, practicing it, and performing it?

Ave Maria
(Angelus Domini)

Franz Biebl

Trio*, SATB, Mixed Chorus, SATB, A cappella

* A small ensemble may be used.

2. Tenor Solo

mp

Et ver-bum ca-ro fac-tum est et ha-bi-ta-vit___ in no-bis.

Return to measure 1

22 3.

-sus. Sanc-ta Ma-ri-a, ma-ter De-i,

-sus. Sanc-ta Ma-ri-a, ma-ter De-i, o-ra pro

27

o-ra pro no-bis pec-ca-to-ri-bus. Sanc-ta Ma-

no-bis pec-ca-to-ri-bus. Sanc-ta Ma-ri-a,

Making Historical Connections

The perfection of Leonardo da Vinci's (1452–1519) *Ginevra de' Benci* is achieved by exacting attention to detail, including the study of human anatomy. Attention to a balanced distribution of voice parts progressing in a calm, smooth momentum, expresses Renaissance musical style.

c. 1474. *Ginevra de' Benci*. Leonardo da Vinci. Oil on panel. 38.8 x 36.7 cm (15 ¼ x 14 ½"). National Gallery of Art, Washington, D.C. Ailsa Mellon Bruce Fund.

Renaissance Period

After completing this lesson, you will be able to:

- *Discuss some of the major changes that took place in Europe during the Renaissance.*
- *Describe the most important characteristics of Renaissance music.*
- *Identify the major forms of sacred and secular music during the Renaissance.*
- *Discuss the most important characteristics of Renaissance choral music.*

Early in the fifteenth century, a "rebirth" began in Europe—a renewal of creative activity, of intellectual curiosity, and of artistic development. This was the beginning of the Renaissance, a period that takes its name from the old French word *renaistre*, meaning "to be born again."

Changes During the Renaissance

The Renaissance was a time of growth, experimentation, and discovery in many fields. Scholars retreated from an acceptance of what they read; instead, they began using observation and experimentation to draw new conclusions about the world around them. The results of this new approach were a series of important advances in science, mathematics, and technology.

The Renaissance also saw important advances in exploration and trade. For the first time, European sailing ships reached the southern coast of Africa, the Americas, and India, and even succeeded in sailing around the world. These journeys brought a new expanding sense of the world, an influx of new ideas, and new opportunities for trade to the people of Renaissance Europe.

A particularly significant development of the Renaissance was the invention of a printing press with movable type, usually credited to Johann Gutenberg. This press meant that books no longer had to be copied by hand. Books—including books about music and books of music—became much less expensive and much more widely available; reading words and reading music were no longer pursuits restricted to the wealthy, privileged few.

Changes in religious practice and belief were also important during the Renaissance. The Catholic church, which had been a center of learning, a formidable political power, and an important force in the daily lives of nearly all Europeans, gradually lost some of its influence. The foremost Renaissance scholars embraced humanism, a belief in the dignity and value of individual human beings. In addition, the Protestant Reformation resulted in the establishment of new Christian churches not under the rule of the Catholic hierarchy.

The visual arts of the Renaissance reflect the era's growing awareness of the natural world. The human figures depicted by painters and sculptors became more realistic and more individualized.

CHORAL MUSIC TERMS

a cappella
Gregorian chant
madrigal
mass
motet
motive imitation
polyphony
sacred music
secular music

1453

Ottoman Turks capture Constantinople, marking end
of Byzantine Empire

Every aspect of the dome of St. Peter's by Michelangelo Buonarroti (1475–1564) contributes to the impression of an upward thrust of energy. The ribs, buttresses, and supports of the dome bear a relationship to the borrowed plainsong melodies that support religious music composed during the Renaissance.

1546–64. Dome of St. Peter's Basilica, view from the southwest. Michelangelo Buonarroti. (Completed by Giacomo della Porta in 1590.) Vatican State, Rome, Italy.

Da Vinci sketches an early helicopter design   Columbus lands in West Indies/Americas

▼ **1483**   ▼ **1492**

▲ **1473-1480**   ▲ **1488**   ▲ **1498**
Sistine Chapel built   Diaz sails around the Cape of Good Hope   Da Gama sails around Africa
                                                                           and lands in India

Although many paintings and sculptures depicted religious subjects, nonreligious subjects, especially those taken from Greek and Roman mythology, became increasingly acceptable. Artists also created individual portraits, such as the famous *Mona Lisa* by Leonardo da Vinci. New materials and new techniques enhanced the artists' ability to create lifelike works.

Renaissance Music

Throughout the Renaissance, the Catholic church continued to exert a strong influence on the arts. Much of the important music composed during this period was **sacred music,** *music used in religious services.*

In the centuries preceding the Renaissance—the Middle Ages—the most important musical form was the **Gregorian chant,** *a melody sung in unison by male voices.* All these chants were sung **a cappella,** *without instrumental accompaniment.* The earliest Gregorian chants consisted of a single melodic line; later, a second melodic line was added. This addition was the beginning of **polyphony,** *the simultaneous performance of two or more melodic lines.* In polyphonic music, each part begins at a different place, and each part is independent and important. The sacred music of the Renaissance grew from the medieval Gregorian chants. The use of polyphony was extended and developed by Renaissance composers; and although instrumentation was added to many sacred works, the Renaissance is often called the golden age of a cappella choral music.

The two major forms of sacred Renaissance music were the **mass,** *a long musical composition that includes the five major sections of the Catholic worship service*, and the **motet,** *a shorter choral work set to Latin texts and used in religious services, but not part of the regular mass.*

John Dunstable was one of the foremost composers of Renaissance masses and motets. His works show new developments in the harmonic structure of polyphony. Later, Josquin Desprez introduced homophonic harmonies, produced by chords that support a melody. He was also one of the first to compose works with **motive imitation,** *short repeating melodies between voice parts.*

Although many sacred works of the period were sung a cappella, instruments were added in other compositions to accompany and echo the voice parts. Composers such as Adrian Willaert combined voices, pipe organs, and other instruments in sacred music.

Sacred music for Protestant services was also written during the Renaissance. Martin Luther, one of the most important leaders of the Protestant Reformation, wrote hymns that are still sung in Protestant churches today.

There were also changes in **secular music,** *any music that is not sacred.* As secular music gained in importance and popularity, the center of musical activity began to shift from churches to castles and towns.

Sistine Chapel ceiling painted by
Michelangelo

1508

Cortez conquers Mexico

1519

1517

Protestant Reformation begins in Germany
with Luther's 95 Theses

1519

Magellan begins voyage around the world

The **madrigal,** *a secular form written in several imitative parts*, became the most popular kind of nonsacred composition during the Renaissance. Composers including Clement Janequin, Heinrich Isaac, Thomas Tallis, William Byrd, Thomas Morley, and Thomas Weelkes wrote madrigals to be sung by everyday people; singing madrigals together was an important entertainment during this period.

Characteristics of Choral Music During the Renaissance

Most of the music of the Renaissance was choral; instruments were used primarily as accompaniment. The choral music of the time can be considered in terms of its meter and stress, tempo, dynamics, texture, expressive aspects, and tone quality.

Meter and stress as we know them were not introduced into choral music until after the Renaissance period. Renaissance works lacked a clearly defined beat. Instead, choral works had a gently flowing rhythm. This rhythm often varied among the melodic lines, creating a special challenge for singers of Renaissance compositions. Renaissance works were generally sung at a moderate tempo, without any unusual shifts from one tempo to another.

The dynamics of most Renaissance choral compositions were moderate and steady; there were typically no major shifts from loud to soft or soft to loud.

The texture of Renaissance choral music was primarily polyphonic. The separate voices within a work—as many as six voice parts—usually conveyed equal melodic interest. In general, the music of the period had a fuller, richer sound than did compositions from the Middle Ages.

The expressive aspects of choral music reflected the attitudes of the Renaissance: rational, balanced, and emotionally restrained. Many of the sacred works were intended not only to enhance religious worship but also to strengthen the influence of the Church.

Sacred choral works were performed with men and boys singing all the voice parts, although women participated in singing many madrigals. The tone quality was generally restrained, with little or no vibrato.

Elizabeth I crowned Queen of England
(died 1603)

▼ 1558

William Shakespeare begins play writing

▼ c. 1590

▲ 1584
Sir Walter Raleigh discovers Virginia

▲ 1599
Globe Theatre built in London

Check Your Understanding

Recall

1. Why was the invention of a printing press with movable type such an important development during the Renaissance?

2. What is the difference between sacred music and secular music?

3. What is a Gregorian chant?

4. What is polyphony?

5. What is the difference between a mass and a motet?

6. What is a madrigal? How is it different from a motet?

7. What kind of tempo is typical of Renaissance choral music?

8. What kind of texture do most Renaissance choral works have?

Thinking It Through

1. Identify and describe a Renaissance choral work you have heard. In what ways is that work characteristic of the period?

2. What relationships can you identify between Renaissance music and music that is being composed and performed now? Explain your ideas.

Listening to . . .

Renaissance Music

CHORAL SELECTION

Desprez — "Ave Maria"

Josquin Desprez was a Flemish Renaissance composer. He was born about the year 1440 and died 1521. He enjoyed an international career and spent much of his time in Italy. His music strongly influenced later composers.

The motet "Ave Maria" is an a cappella choral work set to a sacred Latin text that is not part of the main mass of the Catholic church. It was often used at vesper services at sunset. "Ave Maria" is a four-voice setting of a Latin prayer to the Virgin Mary.

INSTRUMENTAL SELECTION

Dowland — "The Most Sacred Queen Elizabeth, Her Galliard"

John Dowland (1563–1626) was a well-known English Renaissance composer and lutenist. He published eight books of music during his lifetime. As a court musician to the minor aristocracy and to the King of Denmark, he wrote many secular works—both songs and instrumental—as well as sacred pieces. Although his compositions were very popular with the middle class, it was not until five years before his death that he was recognized by the English Court and appointed as one of the King's Lutes to the Court of England.

A *galliard* is a composition written for social dancing. Galliards from the period 1590 to 1625 were plentiful and have a musical substance and interest far beyond the needs of functional dance music. Those written for keyboard and lute often display considerable brilliance. Each strain is followed by a variation enlivened by scales, runs, and other kinds of figuration, instead of a customary repetition of the strain. The use of *hemiola* is one consistent feature of the galliard throughout most of its history.

RENAISSANCE CONNECTIONS

Introducing...
"Ave Regina Coelorum"

Orlande de Lassus

Setting the Stage

"Row, Row, Row Your Boat" is a round song that children learn to sing at an early age. Did you know that a performance of this type of song results in music characteristics that go back over 500 years? We say that a round has linear texture. In other words, the different voice parts move independently in order to form the chordal structure of the song. The selection you will sing, "Ave Regina Coelorum," has this same linear texture, although it is not a round. As you listen to the selection, you will notice that the other voice parts all have rhythms and melodies that move at different times, yet the overall sound is pleasing to the ear. This sacred piece is very typical of Renaissance music. You will find the syllables and words that are very connected to the phrases, or musical thoughts and sentences. Once you have mastered the notes, see how well you and your fellow choir members can define the phrase and bring out the different voice parts—similarly to singing "Row, Row, Row, Your Boat."

Meeting the Composer
Orlande de Lassus

Orlande de Lassus (1532–1594), also known as Orlando di Lasso, was the last of the composers from the Netherlands who dominated European music for more than a hundred years. At a young age, he began to sing in church choirs. At the age of 12, he went to Italy, where he sang in and directed choirs for more than 10 years. De Lassus wrote sacred motets, masses, and hundreds of shorter sacred works for voices. He also wrote French chansons, Italian madrigals, and German part songs. He composed more than two thousand works!

Ave Regina Coelorum

COMPOSER: *Orlande de Lassus (Orlando di Lasso) (1532–1594)*
TRANSLATOR: *John Colman*
EDITED BY: *Clifford Richter*

CHORAL MUSIC TERMS

breathing

part independence

polyphony

posture

Renaissance

rhythm

syncopation

VOICING

SATB

PERFORMANCE STYLE

Moderate tempo

A cappella

FOCUS

- Sing with correct posture and good breath support.
- Read and perform rhythms including syncopation, eighth-sixteenth combinations, and dotted quarter-eighth note patterns.
- Read and sing one part independently when four parts are sung in polyphonic texture.
- Sing using correct Latin pronunciation.

Warming Up

Vocal Warm-Up

To inhale, imagine being astonished, and feel your whole body suddenly opening, as the air literally falls into your lungs. To exhale, pretend that you are quieting a group by saying "psst" at varying lengths. Now sing the following exercise on *ho* to strengthen the diaphragm. Move up by half steps on each repeat.

Ho ho ho ho   ho ho ho ho   ho.   Ho ho ho ho   ho ho ho ho   ho.

Sight-Singing

Read and clap the following rhythm in four parts. Can you clap all parts accurately the first time through? Notice the syncopated rhythms created by ties. Sing your voice part rhythm, using chord tones from one of the following chords: G major, G minor, D major, D VII, or C major. Repeat the activity using a different chord, or assign different chords to each measure of rhythm.

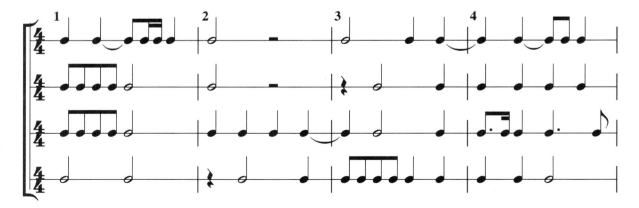

Singing: "Ave Regina Coelorum"

"Row, Row, Row Your Boat" is a round you probably learned as a child. A round has linear texture, with different voice parts moving independently to create the chordal structure of the song. Rounds, canons, and polyphony began more than 500 years ago, during the Renaissance period. Each voice part has melody and rhythm that move at different times, yet the overall sound is pleasing to the ear. Repeatedly a voice part imitates the rhythm or melody of the one before it, weaving vocal lines into polyphonic texture.

Now turn to the music for "Ave Regina Coelorum" on page 158.

HOW DID YOU DO?

? ? ?

Your good technique will help to bring out the best in Renaissance style. Think about your preparation and performance of "Ave Regina Coelorum."

1. Did you use correct posture and breathing? How would the observer know? What would they see? What do you feel?

2. Could you read the rhythms and pitches of the piece? What was easy? What needed practice?

3. Was your Latin pronunciation correct? What was good? What could be better?

4. Describe the characteristics of this piece that indicate its origins in the Renaissance period, and tell how you enhanced these characteristics through your performance.

Ave Regina Coelorum
Thou Art the Queen of All Heaven

Four-part Chorus of Mixed Voices
A cappella

Orlande de Lassus (Orlando di Lasso) (1532–1594)
Edited by Clifford Richter
English version by John Colman

All tempo, dynamic, and expression marks are editorial additions, as are the bar lines and time signature. Editorial accidentals have been placed in square brackets, cautionary accidentals in parentheses.

© Copyright 1963 by Associated Music Publishers, Inc., New York

In *The Return of the Prodigal Son,* **Bartolomé Esteban Murillo (1617–1682) expresses the attitude of the Catholic church during the Counter-Reformation, hoping to welcome back the followers of Martin Luther (1483–1546). To the contrary, a significant body of religious music was created to serve the new form of worship in the Protestant churches.**

1667–70. *The Return of the Prodigal Son.* (Detail.) Bartolomé Esteban Murillo. Oil on canvas. 236.3 x 261.0 cm (93 x 102 ³/₄"). National Gallery of Art, Washington, D.C. Gift of the Avalon Foundation.

Baroque Period

After completing this lesson, you will be able to:

- Discuss some of the major changes that took place in Europe during the Baroque period.
- Describe the most important characteristics of Baroque music.
- Identify at least three musical forms that developed during the Baroque period.
- Discuss the most important characteristics of Baroque choral music.

The balance and restraint of the Renaissance period were followed by an era in which all the arts, including music, became more emotional, dramatic, and decorative: the Baroque period.

Changes During the Baroque Period

The explorations and developments undertaken during the Renaissance period continued and expanded during the Baroque period. European navigators, explorers, traders, and settlers traveled to other parts of the world, and the first colonies were established in the Americas. Science and mathematics also expanded; scholars used new instruments and new insights to develop specialized fields of study.

The paintings, sculpture, and architecture of the Baroque period reflect society's interests in flamboyance and dramatic detail. Many were created as displays of the wealth and splendor of European emperors, kings, and other power aristocrats. Elaborate palaces, surrounded by vast formal gardens and decorated with large-scale and dramatic paintings and sculpture, typified the artistic intentions of the Baroque period. Baroque painters, including Caravaggio, Rubens, Rembrandt, and Velazquez, brought dramatic new effects to their works. The sculptors of the period, especially Bernini and Borromini, created pieces with a new sense of movement. Drama and emotional effects—and eventually flamboyance—were emphasized in the visual artworks of the Baroque period.

Baroque Music

Like the visual artworks of the time, Baroque music was characterized by complex details and new emotional content. Many works were composed with a strong sense of movement and a highly ornamental melody. One important musical feature developed during this period was the **continuo,** *a continually moving bass line.* Another was the use of improvisation; musicians often improvised additional melodic ornamentations during performances.

Instrumental music gained in importance during the Baroque period. Two major instrumental forms developed. The **concerto grosso** is *a composition for a small chamber orchestra consisting of several movements and featuring a bass line and an elaborate melody.* The Baroque concerto grosso

COMPOSERS

Claudio Monteverdi (1567–1643)
Arcangelo Corelli (1643–1713)
Henry Purcell (1659–1695)
Antonio Vivaldi (1678–1741)
Johann Sebastian Bach (1685–1750)
George Frideric Handel (1685–1759)
Giovanni Battista Pergolesi (1710–1736)

ARTISTS

El Greco (1541–1614)
Michelangelo da Caravaggio (c. 1565–1609)
Peter Paul Rubens (1577–1640)
Frans Hals (1580–1666)
Artemisia Gentileschi (1593–1653)
Gianlorenzo Bernini (1598–1680)
Francesco Borromini (1599–1667)
Rembrandt van Rijn (1606–1669)
Judith Leyser (1609–1660)
Bartolomé Esteban Murillo (1617–1682)

AUTHORS

John Donne (c. 1573–1631)
René Descartes (1596–1650)
John Milton (1608–1674)
Molière (1622–1673)

CHORAL MUSIC TERMS

cantata
chorale
concerto grosso
continuo
opera
oratorio
recitative
suite
terraced dynamics

Galileo | Henry Hudson explores the Hudson River | Pilgrims land in America | Isaac Newton | Quakers arrive in Massachusetts

1564-1642 | **1609** | **1620** | **1642-1727** | **1656**

1607 | **1618-1648** | **1636** | **1643-1715**
Jamestown, Virginia, established settlement | Thirty Years' War | Harvard College founded | Reign of Louis XIV, as King of France

1608
Telescope invented

features interplay between a small group of soloists and the larger group of players. The contrast between the small and large groups, between the soft and loud sounds, is one of the key features of Baroque music.

Another important new instrumental form was the **suite,** *a set of musical movements, usually inspired by dances, of contrasting tempos and styles.* Suites were written for solo instruments, for small instrumental groups, and for complete orchestras.

One of the most characteristic developments of the Baroque period was the **opera,** *a combination of singing, instrumental music, dancing, and drama that tells a story.* Claudio Monteverdi composed *Orfeo,* the first important opera, in 1607. The most famous English composer of the period, Henry Purcell, wrote the opera *Dido and Aeneas* in 1689.

In replacing symmetry and balance with the ornate and intricate, Balthazar Neumann, in the Nave of Vierzehnheiligen Pilgrim Church, expressed the distinction between Renaissance and Baroque style in both art and music. Complexity and ornamentation are prevalent characteristics of music in the Baroque period, in contrast to the calm, smooth style of the Renaissance.

1743–72. The Nave of Vierzehnheiligen Pilgrim Church. Balthazar Neumann. Vierzehnheiligen Pilgrim Church, near Bamberg, West Germany.

Although the Baroque period is noted for its rise in the importance of instrumental music, there were also significant developments in vocal music. The **cantata** was *a collection of compositions with instrumental accompaniment consisting of several movements based on related secular or sacred text segments.* The fact that this form could be composed either as a sacred or as a secular work was, in itself, an innovation. The **chorale** was *a hymn tune, generally composed for Protestant worship services with German texts.* Chorales were intended to be easy to sing and to remember so that all members of a church congregation could join in.

The third major vocal development was closely related to opera, but without the acting, costumes, and scenery. The **oratorio** was *a composition for solo voices, chorus, and orchestra that was an extended dramatic work on a literary or religious theme presented without theatrical action.* An oratorio was typically performed by a small chorus, an orchestra, and four solo voices. Though most oratorios recount religious stories, they were not intended to be part of a religious service.

Johann Sebastian Bach

1685–1750

First American newspaper
established, *Boston News Letter*   Handel comes to England

1704   **1710**

1682   **1685–1759**   **1706–1790**

LaSalle explores   George Frideric Handel   Benjamin Franklin
the Mississippi

1687

Publication of Newton's *Mathematical Principles*

Characteristics of Choral Music During the Baroque Period

Like all forms of Baroque music, the choral works of the period were more dramatic and emotional than the vocal music of the Renaissance. The developments of the period can be considered in terms of the meter and stress, tempo, dynamics, texture, and expressive aspects of Baroque choral music.

The Baroque period saw the introduction of metered music; music was organized and notated in regular groups of beats. The accents within these groups came at regular intervals. Typically, weak beats led into stronger beats, and short notes led into longer notes in choral works of the time. The **recitative,** *a vocal line in an oratorio or a cantata (or opera) that imitates the rhythm of speech,* moved the focus to textual declamation.

The tempo of Baroque choral music was generally moderate. A steady, unflagging rhythm is considered a major characteristic in choral works of the time. In many works, the tempo is held back slightly as one melodic phrase concludes and before the next section begins. Such variations and pauses were often used to heighten the emotional quality of a work. By the end of the seventeenth century, the Italian words used to indicate tempo at the beginning of a piece (*largo, allegro,* and *presto,* for example) had come into general use.

Within the dynamics of choral music, extremes were generally avoided during the Baroque period. **Terraced dynamics**—*a rather abrupt alteration between loud and soft*—were most common; crescendo and decrescendo were not frequently used. Instrumentation became more important in choral works; rather than simply doubling the voices, instruments began to "accompany" the singers.

Check Your Understanding

Recall

1. How were the visual artworks of the Baroque period different from those of the Renaissance period?

2. How did Baroque musicians use improvisation?

3. What is a suite?

4. What is a cantata? On what kinds of text were Baroque cantatas based?

5. What is an oratorio? How is it similar to and different from an opera?

6. What kind of tempo did most Baroque choral works have?

Thinking It Through

1. Based on what you have read and what you have heard, which do you prefer—Renaissance choral music or Baroque choral music? Why?

2. Choose any form of popular music you enjoy listening to. Explain the similarities and differences between that music and the choral music of the Baroque Period.

Listening to . . .
Baroque Music

CHORAL SELECTION

Bach — *Cantata No. 140,* Fourth Movement, Chorale

Johann Sebastian Bach (1685–1750) was a German composer and organist, the youngest son of a town musician. He wrote music of all genres including vocal, instrumental, and keyboard/organ. He wrote over 200 church cantatas, one of the most famous being *Cantata No. 140* (1731). In the fourth movement, "Zion hort die Wachter singen," Bach utilizes a chorale as the "cantus firmus," using a free ritornello to separate the phrases of the chorale melody.

INSTRUMENTAL SELECTION

Vivaldi — *La Primavera,* First Movement

Antonio Vivaldi (1678–1741) was an Italian composer. He is best known as the master of concertos, having written over 500, half of them for solo violin and orchestra. His most well-known work is *The Four Seasons*. It is a set of four solo concertos for violin, string orchestra, and basso continuo. As programmatic music, each portrays one of the seasons of the year, corresponding with sonnets that preface each concerto.

Introducing . . .

"Alleluia"

Giovanni Battista Pergolesi

Setting the Stage

While not specified in this edition of "Alleluia," this piece by Pergolesi is most likely a larger part of a larger work, perhaps from a setting of the mass. The piece is very reflective of the mature Baroque style in the use of sequences as a compositional technique and as an example of the now clearly defined major-minor harmonic system.

Meeting the Composer
Giovanni Battista Pergolesi

Giovanni Battista Pergolesi (1710–1736) was one of the northern Italian composers known as the "Neapolitans." His style reflected an attempt to offer the audience music that was clear, simple, and pleasant to hear. From these ideals came the beginnings of what we now call the Classical period. The Neapolitans also used more chromaticism (moving in half steps) in their music, affecting both the melodies and harmonies. Pergolesi wrote a musical setting of the *Stabat Mater* (a liturgical text from the thirteenth century, "By the Cross the Mother Standing" referring to Mary, the Mother of Jesus), which shows the delicate texture, the very balanced phrasing, and the lyrical tone of Italian sacred music of this time period. He also composed instrumental pieces and serious operas. His opera buffa (comic opera), *La serva padrona* (The Maid Mistress, 1733), established Pergolesi as the first master of this new style.

Alleluía

COMPOSER: *Giovanni Battista Pergolesi* (1710–1736)

EDITED BY: *Hubert Bird*

CHORAL MUSIC TERMS

Baroque

melodic imitation

melodic sequences

part independence

polyphony

VOICING

SSATB

PERFORMANCE STYLE

Strongly, boldly

A cappella

FOCUS

- Read and sing one part when five parts are sung in polyphony.
- Identify and sing melodic imitation.
- Identify and perform melodic sequences.

Warming Up

Vocal Warm-Up

Read and sing this exercise with good energy, closing quickly to the "l" on the first two syllables. Move upward in scalewise steps on each repeat. When you sing the same melodic pattern beginning on different pitches each time, it is called a sequence.

Sight-Singing

Sight-sing this exercise using solfège and hand signs or numbers. Try a variety of voicings, for example: S/A sing part I, T/B sing part II, S/T sing part I, A/B sing part II. Support the higher pitches with plenty of breath. Notice the sequences in each part line and the imitative rhythms between parts.

Singing: "Alleluia"

Imagine a Slinky™ toy descending down stairs, step by step. Each motion has the same pattern, but begins one step lower than the one before. A melodic sequence resembles the toy. Once a pattern is established, it is repeated, beginning either higher or lower than the previous pattern.

Echo some melodic patterns. Now, instead of echoing, create a melodic sequence by singing the pattern two more times, one step higher or lower on each repeat, keeping the same pitch relationships intact.

Now turn to the music for "Alleluia" on page 172.

HOW DID YOU DO?

?
?

By now, you know the sequence for learning and preparing a piece of music for performance. Think about your preparation and performance of "Alleluia."

1. Can you read and sing your voice part when four other parts are being sung? What makes it easy or difficult in this particular piece?

2. Describe melodic imitation between voices, and point out where it occurs in "Alleluia."

3. Describe melodic sequences, point them out in the Sight-Singing exercise, then sing the exercise with one or three classmates, to demonstrate how they sound.

4. Describe the characteristics of this piece that indicate its origins in the Baroque period, and tell how you enhanced these characteristics through your performance.

To Al Thrasher

Alleluía

Giovanni Battista Pergolesi (1710–1736)
Edited by Hubert Bird

Five-part Chorus of Mixed Voices,
(SSATB) A cappella

*The original is a whole tone lower and *alle breve.*

Cornelia Pointing to Her Children as Her Treasures,
by Angelica Kauffmann (1741–1807), focuses on
one subject, avoiding details that might distract
from the simple statement. Haydn and Mozart, as
composers of the Classical period, also focused on
the importance of a composition's musical theme
and its clarity, avoiding distracting details.

1785. *Cornelia Pointing to Her Children as Her Treasures.* (Detail.) Angelica Kauffmann.
Oil on canvas. 101.6 x 127.0 cm (40 x 50"). Virginia Museum of Fine Arts,
Richmond, Virginia. The Adolph D. and Wilkins C. Williams Fund, 1975.

Classical Period

After completing this lesson, you will be able to:

- Discuss some of the major changes that took place in Europe and the Americas during the Classical period.
- Describe the most important characteristics of Classical music.
- Identify the most important composers of the Classical period.
- Discuss the most important characteristics of Classical choral music.

The Baroque period, characterized by the emotion, drama, and opulence of its artworks, was followed by the Classical period, in which the arts focused on standards of balance, clarity, and simplicity. Scholars and artists of the period looked back to the works and attitudes of ancient Greece and Rome and adopted as new the ideals they saw reflected in ancient times.

Changes During the Classical Period

The Classical period is often called the Age of Enlightenment. The people of this era put their faith in reason and thought, not in tradition and emotion. This focus on reason resulted in political upheaval and in a return to more restrained, less emotional artistic expression.

The most important political events of the Classical period brought major changes to specific countries and affected the attitudes and ideas of people in other parts of Europe and the Americas. The American colonists revolted against their British rulers and succeeded in founding an independent nation, the United States of America. Several years later, the French Revolution began; this uprising established a new government and confirmed a new societal structure in France.

The visual artists of the Classical period emulated the balance and grandeur they saw in the surviving works from ancient Greece and Rome. This influence can be seen directly in the subjects chosen by painters such as Jacques Louis David, in the heroic yet individualized works by sculptors such as Jean Antoine Houdon, and in the clear Roman elements of structures such as the Brandenburg Gate in Berlin and Monticello, Thomas Jefferson's home in Virginia.

Classical Music

The music of the Classical period left behind the extreme drama and emotion of Baroque compositions, with their exaggerated embellishments and improvisations. Instead, Classical compositions emphasized precision and balance. An essential characteristic of the period was a careful balance between the content of the music and the form in which the music was expressed.

COMPOSERS

Franz Joseph Haydn (1732–1809)
Wolfgang Amadeus Mozart (1756–1791)
Ludwig van Beethoven (1770–1827)
Vincento Bellini (1801–1835)

ARTISTS

Francois Boucher (1703–1770)
Jean-Honoré Fragonard (1732–1806)
Angelica Kauffmann (1741–1807)
Jean Antoine Houdon (1741–1828)
Francisco Gôya (1746–1828)
Jacques Louis David (1748–1825)

AUTHORS

Jonathan Swift (1667–1745)
Samuel Richardson (1689–1761)
Voltaire (1694–1778)
Henry Fielding (1707–1754)
Wolfgang Goethe (1749–1832)
Friedrich von Schiller (1759–1805)
Jane Austen (1775–1817)

CHORAL MUSIC TERMS
chamber music
sonata-allegro form
string quartets
symphony

Swift's *Gulliver's Travels* published

1726

George Washington

1732–1799

Thomas Jefferson

1743–1826

American Revolutionary War fought

1775–1783

1732–1757

Franklin writes *Poor Richard's Almanac*

1775

James Watt invents the steam engine

▲ **The state capitol of Virginia demonstrates the interest of eighteenth-century artists in the simplicity of Greco-Roman design. Attention to clean, simple forms dominate the music of the late eighteenth century as well.**

1785–96. State Capitol of Virginia. Thomas Jefferson. Richmond, Virginia.

Two composers dominated the period: Wolfgang Amadeus Mozart and Franz Joseph Haydn. A third major composer of the time, Ludwig van Beethoven, belongs both to the Classical period and to the next era, the Romantic period. Beethoven's compositions began in the Classical style, but the texture, emotion, and new forms of his later music belong more to the Romantic period.

The most important Classical developments came in instrumental music, which continued to gain in importance. Probably the greatest contribution of this period was the **symphony,** *a large-scale piece for orchestra in three or more movements.* A Classical symphony usually consisted of four movements in the following order: 1) A dramatic, fast movement; 2) A slow movement, often in sonata form; 3) A dance-style movement; 4) An exciting, fast movement.

The Classical period also saw a rise in the popularity of **chamber music,** *music composed for a small group of instruments and designed to be played in a room (or chamber) rather than in a concert hall.* These works are generally light and entertaining, both for the performers and for the listeners. The most popular Classical chamber music compositions were **string quartets,** *pieces composed for two violins, a viola, and a cello.*

Another important instrumental development was the **sonata-allegro form,** *a movement written in AA'BA form.* The sonata-allegro form opens with a single theme (A). Then that theme is repeated with elaboration (A') and followed by a contrasting development (B). The sonata-allegro form closes with a return to the original theme (A).

In general, the vocal and mixed forms of the Baroque period were continued in the Classical period, but with new interpretations that emphasized on balance and elegance.

Characteristics of Choral Music During the Classical Period

Like other compositions of the time, the choral works of the Classical period upheld the standards of simplicity and clarity. These standards were reflected in the meter and stress, tempo, dynamics, texture, and expressive aspects of Classical choral music.

An important characteristic of Classical choral compositions was a definite sense of meter. These works generally had a clear pulsation, but it was more delicate than

American Declaration of Independence signed

1776

Federal Government established in America

1789

1789

French Revolution begins

1808

Roman excavations begin at Pompeii, Italy

that heard in Baroque choral works. Choral works of the period usually exhibited a moderate tempo, free from any extremes. Composers became more likely to mark their scores with tempo indications, providing a clear direction for performers. The metronome was invented early in the nineteenth century and helped stabilize the tempo of choral performances. After about 1816, composers were able to mark the specific metronome numbers, showing the exact number of beats per minute, for each section of a composition.

The terraced dynamics of the Baroque period were generally replaced by gradual crescendo and decrescendo in Classical choral works. Audiences considered these gradual changes from loud to soft and from soft to loud an exciting innovation.

Among the expressive aspects of Classical choral music were a clearly defined structure and characteristic emphasis on symmetry, balance, clarity, and restraint. Music ornamentation continued to be featured in choral music, although it was more refined and restrained than in works of the late Baroque period. Although many choral works included emotional content, the emotion was expressed less dramatically and with greater detachment than in Baroque works.

Check Your Understanding

Recall

1. What were the two most important political events of the Classical period?

2. Who were the two most important composers of the Classical period?

3. What is a symphony? What four movements did a Classical symphony usually include?

4. What is chamber music? What was the main characteristic of most Classical chamber works?

5. What is a sonata-allegro form?

6. What kind of tempo was typical of Classical choral works?

7. What were the major features of Classical choral dynamics?

8. How was the tone quality of Classical choral music different from that of Baroque choral music?

Thinking It Through

1. How is Classical choral music similar to Renaissance choral music? What are the major differences?

2. Identify a Classical choral work you have heard. Discuss the meter and stress, the tempo, the dynamics, the texture, the expressive aspects, and the tone quality of the work.

Listening to...
Classical Music

CHORAL SELECTION

Mozart — "Dies Irae" from *Requiem*

Mozart was born in Salzburg, Austria, in 1756. He died at the early age of 35 in the year 1791. Mozart was gifted as both a performer and a composer. His father began taking him on performance tours when Mozart was just six years old, and by the time he was 12, Mozart had composed his first symphony, oratorio, and opera. Although he died just before his thirty-sixth birthday, Mozart composed more than 600 works, including symphonies, concertos, sonatas, and operas. The *Requiem* is one of the last pieces written by Mozart. It was left unfinished at his death.

A *requiem* is a service in the Catholic church that honors the dead. A requiem such as this would only be performed at the funeral of very important people because of the length and the skill required. Sometimes it is now performed on All Saints Day (First Sunday in November) in remembrance of those who have died.

INSTRUMENTAL SELECTION

Mozart — Piano Concerto No. 23 in A Major: First Movement

Wolfgang Amadeus Mozart (1756–1791) was an Austrian composer and child prodigy. He wrote a number of compositions in his short lifespan for all genres—symphonies, operas, masses, and keyboard and solo instruments, both secular and sacred. *Piano Concerto in A Major* was composed during one of Mozart's more productive and successful times in his life. It is in three movements and follows the traditional sonata concerto form.

Introducing...

"Come, Lovely Spring"

Franz Joseph Haydn

Setting the Stage

Do you like to dance? How often have you heard a popular song whose beat just impelled you to dance? Just like many of our current songs today, this one will capture your intrinsic desire to move and sway to the music. It lilts in a steady unflagging tempo from beginning to end with lightness and simplicity. The number is typically classical, but fresh as a springtime morning. In fact, have you ever sung an arrangement of the song "Morning Has Broken"? What a wonderful piece this would be preceding a performance of "Come, Lovely Spring." Perhaps you can think of other more current songs that would even fit better. Enjoy!

Meeting the Composer

Franz Joseph Haydn (1732–1809)

Franz Joseph Haydn, Mozart's friend and one of the greatest composers of the Classical period, was born on March 31, 1732, in Ruhr, Austria. Haydn showed an early love of music but did not receive any formal training in composition until his late teens. His works gradually gained recognition, and when he was 29 years old Haydn entered the service of the aristocratic Hungarian Esterhazy family. This patronage provided a steady income and required Haydn to compose work requested by the family and to conduct the court orchestra. Haydn thrived under this system, and he worked diligently. He composed more than 100 symphonies and 68 string quartets, as well as sonatas, operas, oratorios, masses, and other works.

Haydn is well known for taking the already established forms of the symphony and the string quartet and shaping them into the powerful media for musical expression that were recognized by all composers in both the past and the present. Both his masses and his choral works continue as standards in the concert repertory. His operas are also of great musical worth.

Haydn lived from the end of the Baroque period to the beginning of the Romantic period. He led the musical transitions between the two.

Come, Lovely Spring

COMPOSER: *Franz Joseph Haydn (1732–1809)*
TRANSLATORS: *Alice Parker and Thomas Pyle*
EDITED BY: *Robert Shaw*

CHORAL MUSIC TERMS

Classical period

dynamic markings

independent singing

6/8 meter

tempo markings

tempo

VOICING

Four-part chorus

PERFORMANCE STYLE

Allegretto
Accompanied by piano

FOCUS

- Maintain a steady tempo.
- Read and sing accurately in 6/8 meter.
- Sing one part independently when four parts are being sung.
- Identify and interpret Classical dynamic and tempo markings.

Warming Up

Vocal Warm-Up

Read and sing this exercise first using solfège and hand signs or numbers, then on *doo, loo,* or *la.* Move up or down by half steps on each repeat, and maintain a steady beat. As you sing, gently sway from the waist while relaxing arm and neck muscles. This will give you the lilting feeling of 6/8 meter. Repeat this exercise at the end of your Warm-Up session, just before practicing "Come, Lovely Spring."

Sight-Singing

Sight-sing this exercise using solfège and hand signs or numbers. Then sing it in a round, four measures apart, with women beginning, and men adding the second part. This round is not designed for harmonic consonance, but rather to build your vocal independence.

Write the exercise on the board, and then write different tempo and dynamic markings, interpreting them in the Classical style.

Singing: "Come, Lovely Spring"

How do you know what a composer was thinking, especially if he lived from 1732 to 1809? Some of the clues are written down. The notation tells you the rhythms and pitches, and the tempo marking tells you how fast to go.

Dynamic markings are not quite so simple, unless you understand the conventions of the period. In the Classical period, a dynamic marking either indicates a sudden dynamic change, or marks the average dynamic level of each phrase. If this is the case, it is your job to shape the phrase with a crescendo to the peak, and then a release to the end of the phrase. Find the tempo and dynamic markings in "Come, Lovely Spring" so you will be prepared when you sing.

Now turn to the music for "Come, Lovely Spring" on page 186.

HOW DID YOU DO? ? ? ? ?

When you perform, you are the vehicle that brings the music from the composer to the audience. Think about your preparation and performance of "Come, Lovely Spring."

1. Are you able to maintain a steady tempo as you read or perform? Demonstrate by singing the Sight-Singing exercise without any accompaniment.

2. The 6/8 meter should be familiar by now. Are there any rhythms that gave you problems?

3. Are you able to hold your part independently when other parts are being sung? Sing measures 5–30 of "Come, Lovely Spring" with three classmates to demonstrate your ability.

4. Describe the tempo and dynamic markings in "Come, Lovely Spring," and discuss how to interpret them in the style of the Classical period.

5. If Franz Joseph Haydn attended your performance of this piece, what do you suppose he would think of it? What would he like? What might he tell you would improve the performance?

Come, Lovely Spring

(From "The Seasons")

Franz Joseph Haydn (1732–1809)
Edited by Robert Shaw
English Text by
Alice Parker and Thomas Pyle

Four-part Chorus of Mixed Voices
with Piano Accompaniment

No. 2 Chorus

Hay Wain by John Constable (1776–1837) focuses on the natural effect of the sky, including the ever-changing sun, clouds, and wind. These features correlate to an interest in orchestral color, with the symphony orchestra serving as a magnificent palette.

1821. *Hay Wain*. John Constable. Oil on canvas. 1.28 x 1.85 m (4' 2½" x 6' 1"). National Gallery, London, England.

Romantic Period

After completing this lesson, you will be able to:

- Explain the impact of the Industrial Revolution on other developments of the Romantic period.
- Describe the most important characteristics of Romantic music.
- Identify at least four important composers of the Romantic period.
- Discuss the most important characteristics of Romantic choral music.

The restraint of the Renaissance was followed by the more extravagant and emotional Baroque period. After the Baroque period came another time of restraint and balance, the Classical period. Not surprisingly, the Classical period was, in turn, followed by a time of greater emotion and exaggeration: the Romantic period.

Changes During the Romantic Period

One of the most important developments of the Romantic period was the Industrial Revolution. This radical change in manufacturing resulted in many new nonagricultural jobs and contributed to the rapid growth of cities. It also contributed to the growth of the middle class and to a rise in middle-class confidence and influence.

The Industrial Revolution also had a direct impact on changes in music. New techniques resulted in greatly improved musical instruments that could be mass produced. This meant that more musicians were available to perform with better instruments. These changes encouraged composers to exercise their creativity and to take new and more challenging approaches to their work.

The visual artists of the period reflected the era's attitudes with bolder, more colorful works. Landscapes by such Romantic painters as William Turner and John Constable conveyed the movements and feelings of nature. Later, Impressionist painters such as Edouard Manet, Claude Monet, and Pierre Auguste Renoir employed revolutionary techniques to bring the sense of the natural world alive.

Romantic Music

Although Romantic composers continued, in large part, to work with musical forms developed in the past, they used original treatments to create new musical statements. Romantic compositions focused on emotional extremes and were characterized by complexity, exploration, and excitement. The interests of the period were expressed in larger, more complex vocal melodies and more colorful harmonies. In addition, instrumentation was expanded to enhance the overall possibilities of tone color in the music, and rhythms became freer and more flexible.

Many Romantic compositions reflect the period's spirit of **nationalism,** *pride in a country's historical and legendary past.* Composers based both instrumental and vocal works on traditional legends or on

COMPOSERS

Ludwig van Beethoven (1770–1827)
Franz Schubert (1797–1828)
Hector Berlioz (1803–1869)
Felix Mendelssohn (1809–1847)
Frédéric Chopin (1810–1849)
Robert Schumann (1810–1856)
Bedvrich Smetana (1824–1884)
Franz Liszt (1811–1886)
Richard Wagner (1813–1883)
Giuseppe Verdi (1813–1901)
Clara Schumann (1819–1896)
Bedřich Smetana (1824–1884)
Johann Strauss (1825–1899)
Stephen Foster (1826–1864)
Johannes Brahms (1833–1897)
Peter Ilyich Tchaikovsky (1840–1893)
Giacomo Puccini (1858–1924)

ARTISTS

Élisabeth Vigée-Lebrun (1755–1842)
Joseph Mallard William Turner (1775–1851)
John Constable (1776–1837)
Rosa Bonheur (1822–1899)
Edouard Manet (1832–1883)
James A. McNeill Whistler (1834–1903)
Edgar Degas (1834–1917)
Paul Cezanne (1839–1906)
Claude Monet (1840–1926)
Berthe Morisot (1841–1895)
Pierre Auguste Renoir (1841–1919)
Mary Cassatt (1845–1926)
Vincent van Gogh (1853–1890)
Georges Seurat (1859–1891)

AUTHORS

Noah Webster (1758–1843)
Sir Walter Scott (1771–1832)
Mary Wollstonecraft Shelley (1797–1851)
Ralph Waldo Emerson (1803–1882)
Elizabeth Barrett Browning (1806–1861)

CHORAL MUSIC TERMS

art song
nationalism

Louisiana Purchase
transacted
1803

Abraham Lincoln
1809–1865

Frederick Douglass
c.1817–1895

Mary Baker Eddy
1821–1910

1804
Napoleon crowned Emperor

1812–1814
War of 1812

1821
Jean Champollion deciphers Egyptian
hieroglyphics using the Rosetta Stone

1823
Monroe Doctrine created

Although the Belamy Mansion was built during the years designated as the Romantic period, architect Rufus G. Bunnell chose the Classical revival style. The Corinthian columns uphold a monumental cornice and pediment, making a dramatic statement. Similarly, music of the Romantic period was often monumental and dramatic.

1859. The Belamy Mansion, Wilmington, North Carolina. Rufus G. Bunnell.

nationalistic dramas and novels. Operas, particularly the works of Richard Wagner and Giuseppe Verdi, were the most notable musical vehicles of nationalism. Dance music also grew in popularity. Some of these dance compositions reflected the period's nationalism, imitating and echoing traditional folk tunes.

During the Romantic period, instrumental music became more elaborate and overtly expressive. Symphonies gained in popularity. Ludwig van Beethoven—often considered the world's greatest musical genius—expanded the symphony in both length and content. Each of Beethoven's nine symphonies is unique, and all are challenging to the performing musicians. Beethoven's *Ninth Symphony* even includes a chorus and four vocal soloists.

Of the Romantic vocal forms, the most important was the **art song,** *an expressive song about life, love, and human relationships for solo voice and piano.* The German name for these works is *lieder,* and their most famous composers were German-speakers. Austrian Franz Schubert wrote more than 600 songs, as well as symphonies, string quartets, and other works, before his death at the age of 31. German composers Robert Schumann and Johannes Brahms are also known for their *lieder.* The choral music of the Romantic period was characterized by exaggeration and emotion. The flamboyance of these works was expressed in their meter and stress, tempo, dynamics, texture, expressive aspects, and tone quality.

Romantic choral works exhibited contemporary musicians' particular interest in rhythm. Many of these creations were marked by intricate rhythmic patterns and unusual rhythmic surprises. Unlike the choral works of earlier periods, Romantic works

Mary Mason Lyon founds Mt.
Holyoke Female Seminary
▼ 1837

American Civil War
▼ 1861–1865

Wireless telegraph developed by
Guglielmo Marconi
▼ 1895

▲ 1835–1910
Mark Twain

▲ 1844–1900
Friedrich Nietzsche

▲ 1889
Jane Addams and Ellen Starr
found Hull House

▲ 1898
Motion picture camera
patented by Thomas Edison;
sound recording developed

employed extremes in meter tempo, and stress. The changes of tempo within compositions typically reflected changes in mood; often these tempo and mood changes were quite abrupt.

The dynamics of Romantic choral works evidenced extremes as well. Crescendo and decrescendo were widely and expressively used. In many instances, crescendo was combined with a gradual quickening of tempo and decrescendo with a gradual slowing; these combinations heightened the excitement created by choral works. The climax of a work was more likely to be sudden, and accents were employed more frequently. The combination of a large choir and a large orchestra often contributed to a sense of dynamic opulence. The texture of Romantic choral works was often thick, with an emphasis on rich sound. Most works emphasized harmony rather than counterpoint, and there was a new use of chromatic harmony.

In response to the formality and tradition of Classical works, the expressive aspects of Romantic choral works displayed the domination of expression over form. Individual and personal emotion were given free expression, and unusual harmonic, rhythmic, and dynamic effects were frequently used. Composers focused on the use of tone color and the presentation of "singable" melodies. The tone quality of Romantic works also showed the period's reaction against the standards of Classical compositions. There was a return of vibrato to add warmth and emotion to the tone. Tones were varied in response to the mood of the music; in general, however, fullness of tone was emphasized and beauty of tone was considered essential.

Check Your Understanding

Recall

1. How did the Industrial Revolution affect composers of the Romantic period?

2. List at least three adjectives you might use to describe Romantic music.

3. What is nationalism? How was it expressed in Romantic music?

4. What changes did Beethoven make in the composition of symphonies?

5. What is an art song? Name at least two Romantic composers of these works.

6. How did the meter and stress of Romantic choral works differ from those used in Classical choral music?

7. What one quality was typical of Romantic choral works?

Thinking It Through

1. Compare Romantic choral music with Baroque choral music. Discuss the similarities and differences you can identify.

2. To what extent do you think the Romantic period was simply a reaction against the constraints of the Classical period? Which Romantic changes would you consider "action" rather than "reaction"? Explain your ideas.

Listening to . . .

Romantic Music

CHORAL SELECTION

Brahms — *A German Requiem,* Fourth Movement

Johannes Brahms (1833–1897) lived most of his life in Hamburg, Germany. He composed almost every kind of music, except opera, and composed during the Romantic period when music began to move from the more traditional forms as represented by Beethoven to more "discordant" and unusual material as represented by Wagner. Not a religious man, he was moved nonetheless to compose a special work, or *German Requiem*, containing seven movements after the death of his teacher, Robert Schumann, and then of his own mother. The requiem was one of the main genres of choral music during the nineteenth century. Brahms intended to portray death as a time of peace and rest and this "Fourth Movement" was the centerpiece of his beautiful compositional effort. Psalm 84 is the text used for this piece.

INSTRUMENTAL SELECTION

Smetana — "The Moldau"

Bedřich Smetana (1824–1884) was a leading composer of Bohemia (later called Czechoslovakia). Smetana had a passion for music and composed in spite of his father's desire for him to become a lawyer. His musical efforts were mainly focused on trying to produce a Bohemian national music based on the folk songs and dances which already existed. Smetana, awoke one morning to find himself totally deaf, which created a depression that stayed with him through the remainder of his life. "The Moldau" represents Smetana's deep feeling about the beauty and significance of the river that flows through the city of Prague.

♫♪ ROMANTIC CONNECTIONS

Introducing . . .

"So Wahr Die Sonne Scheinet"

Robert Schumann

Setting the Stage

This art song has a strongly Romantic text, using analogies between nature and love, and suggesting that it does not matter what natural disasters may occur, the love between these two people will endure. The structure is deceptively simple and homophonic, but extremely intimate and effective. The use of layering voices, altered tones, melodic skips, and overlapping phrases push the piece always forward. Use of traditional harmonic progressions is applied to the text, suggesting everlasting love, while dissonant and chromatic exploration sneak into the suggestions that nature might fail to be as constant. Dynamics and tempo are critical to successful performance of the piece.

Meeting the Composer

Robert Schumann

Robert Schumann (1810–1856) was a great German Romantic composer. Son of a bookkeeper, he was sent to study law, but instead devoted himself to literature and music. He founded a magazine which explored the most modern trends in the arts, and composed first piano pieces, then art songs, and finally, orchestral pieces. He was intrigued with mystification: secret references hidden in the music that are felt rather than observed by the listener. His literary interest shines through in the settings of Romantic poetry in his art songs. He initially studied piano and later turned to composing. He was a prolific songwriter. In 1840, for example, he wrote over one hundred songs.

So Wahr Die Sonne Scheinet

COMPOSER: *Robert Schumann (1810–1856)*
TRANSLATORS: *Alice and Kurt Bergel*
EDITED BY: *William D. Hall*

CHORAL MUSIC TERMS

dynamic shaping

melodic skips

melodic steps

phrases

Romantic

VOICING

SATB

PERFORMANCE STYLE

Andante
Accompanied by piano

FOCUS

- Sing melodic steps and skips accurately.
- Use dynamics to shape phrases.
- Sing with correct German pronunciation.

Warming Up

Vocal Warm-Up

Sing this exercise on *no*. Move up or down by half steps on each repeat. Give the quarter rest its full value. Notice the melodic steps and skips, and tune each pitch carefully.

No   no . . .

Sight-Singing

Sight-sing this exercise using solfège and hand signs or numbers. First sight-read your part inside your head, then sight-sing in four parts. Can you sing it all the way through the first time? How many phrases are there in this exercise? Where do you think each phrase begins and ends? How will you shape these phrases?

Singing: "So Wahr Die Sonne Scheinet"

What makes a piece of music "Romantic"? The Romantic period was a time of extravagance, exaggeration, and expression. Read the English translation of the text in "So Wahr Die Sonne Scheinet" on page 202. Do you think it is extravagant, exaggerated, or expressive? Explain your answer with examples from the music.

Now sing to the music for "So Wahr Die Sonne Scheinet."

HOW DID YOU DO?

Did you do justice to this Romantic piece? Think about your preparation and performance of "So Wahr Die Sonne Scheinet."
1. How accurately do you sing in tune when other parts are being sung? What makes it more difficult? When is it easy?
2. Discuss the phrasing in "So Wahr Die Sonne Scheinet" and how you shape phrases using dynamics. Demonstrate by singing your voice part in the Sight-Singing exercise.

3. How well did you pronounce the German text?
4. If your ensemble were to get a grade for sight-singing, what would it be? What would your individual grade be? Why?

So Wahr Die Sonne Scheinet

(As Surely as the Sun Shines)

Robert Schumann, Op. 101, No. 8, Edited by William D. Hall

English Text: Alice and Kurt Bergel

SATB and Piano

▲ **The art genre known as Photorealism is well-illustrated in** *Hannah: Who She Is* **by Audrey Flack, (1931–). Throughout her career, Flack has experimented with new techniques, just as contemporary musicians have adopted new techniques for their works. This is a portrait of Flack's daughter, depicted as the goddess-heroine of a Joe Pintauro poem.**

1982. *Hannah: Who She Is.* Audrey Flack. Oil over acrylic on canvas. 213.4 x 152.4 cm (7 x 5'). National Museum of Women in the Arts, Washington, D.C.

After completing this lesson, you will be able to:

- Discuss the importance of the political changes that have taken place during the Contemporary period.
- Describe the effects of technological changes on the musical interests of the public.
- Identify at least four experimental approaches developed during the Contemporary period.
- Discuss some of the characteristics of Contemporary choral music.

Change, experimentation, innovation, and reaction—these have been the central features of life and the arts during the Contemporary period, the time from 1900 until right now.

Changes During the Contemporary Period

The twentieth century has been a time of political change and upheaval. The Contemporary period has seen two world wars; many localized wars; revolutions in Russia, China, and many other countries; the Great Depression; the Cold War; and the rise and fall of Communism in many countries. These political events have brought repeated and often radical changes in the lives and ideas of people around the world.

Predictably, change has been a characteristic of the artworks created during the Contemporary period. Painters have experimented with Expressionism, Fauvism, Nonobjectivism, Cubism, Futurism, Fantasy, Surrealism, Abstract Expressionism, Op Art, Pop Art, and many other styles. Photography has developed as a new and varied art form. Sculptors have created works ranging from abstract to super-real. Architects have worked in such varied materials as steel-and-glass and poured concrete, as well as more traditional brick, stone, and wood.

Contemporary Music

Technological developments during the Contemporary period have had an unusually strong effect on music and on the musical interests of the public. Early in the century, phonographs and records made music readily available to anyone who wanted to hear it. As the century progressed, radio and then television brought news and entertainment—including news about music, live musical performances, and new musical recordings—into most homes. Now tapes, CDs, and computers with interactive software have brought higher quality sounds and images to the public. In addition, synthesizers are making it easier and less expensive for everyone to become involved in making and listening to music.

COMPOSERS

Richard Strauss (1864–1949)
Ralph Vaughan Williams (1872–1958)
Arnold Schoenberg (1874–1951)
Charles Ives (1874–1954)
Béla Bartók (1881–1945)
Igor Stravinsky (1882–1971)
Sergei Prokofiev (1891–1952)
Paul Hindemith (1895–1963)
George Gershwin (1898–1937)
Aaron Copland (1900–1990)
Samuel Barber (1910–1981)
Gian Carlo Menotti (1911–)
Benjamin Britten (1913–1976)
Leonard Bernstein (1918–1990)
Philip Glass (1937–)
André Thomas (unknown)

ARTISTS

Henri Rousseau (1844–1910)
Edvard Munch (1863–1944)
Wassily Kandinsky (1866–1944)
Henri Matisse (1869–1954)
Pablo Picasso (1881–1973)
Georgia O'Keeffe (1887–1986)
Jackson Pollock (1912–1956)
Andrew Wyeth (1917–)
Andy Warhol (1930–1987)
Audrey Flack (1931–)

AUTHORS

George Bernard Shaw (1856–1950)
Sir Arthur Conan Doyle (1859–1930)
Edith Wharton (1862–1937)
Beatrix Potter (1866–1943)
Gertrude Stein (1874–1946)
Robert Frost (1874–1963)

CHORAL MUSIC TERMS
abstract
aleatoric music
dissonance
Expressionism
fusion
Impressionism
twelve-tone music

Wright Brothers' flight

1903

Model T Ford introduced

1908

1905

First motion picture
theater opens

1914–1918

World War I

▲ **The New York Metropolitan Opera House in Lincoln Center, built in the 1960s, blends traditional forms of architecture with a contemporary interest in emphasizing starkness of decoration.**

c. 1960. The New York Metropolitan Opera House, Lincoln Center. New York, New York.

This public involvement in music has encouraged change, experimentation, and innovation. Like visual artists, Contemporary composers have developed many different styles. Most have used and adapted music forms from the Romantic period, including the opera, symphony, and art song, but have adapted those forms to new styles and to new musical ideas. Two major stylistic developments of the century have been **Impressionism,** *works that create a musical picture with a dreamy quality through chromaticism*, and **Expressionism,** *bold and dynamic musical expression of mood with great dissonance.*

First complete talking film

1928

Television begins under the commercial license

1939

First atomic bomb exploded

1945

1927

Lindbergh's solo flight across the Atlantic

1929

New York stock market collapses; Great Depression begins

1939–1945

World War II

1950–1953

Korean War

Many kinds of experimentation have been part of the musical development of the Contemporary period. Some composers have worked in an objective style, emphasizing music for its own sake. Their compositions are **abstract,** *focusing on lines, rows, angles, clusters, textures, and form.*

Contemporary composers have also experimented with **dissonance,** *chords using seconds, fourths, fifths, and sevenths,* rather than with traditional chords built on intervals of a third. These compositions lack a tonal center and a scale-oriented organization of pitch.

Another area of experimentation has been **twelve-tone music.** In this organization, *the twelve tones of the chromatic scale are arranged in a tone row, then the piece is composed by rearranging and arranging the "row" in different ways—backward, forward, in clusters of three or four pitches, and so on.* Many critics consider this approach more satisfying for composers than for listeners.

Composers of the Contemporary period have also experimented with **aleatoric—** or chance**—music,** *works that have only a beginning and an end, with the rest left to chance.* An aleatoric composition usually does have a score, but each performer is given the freedom to make many choices, including which pitch to begin on, how long to hold each pitch, how fast to play, and when to stop playing.

Fusion, *a blending of musical styles,* has been an important part of musical experimentation and change during the Contemporary period. Traditional and folk styles from all parts of the world have blended with each other and with new, popular styles. Popular music and art music have also been blended; pop singers, for example, perform with professional orchestras and choirs, and symphony orchestras perform special arrangements of folk songs.

The Contemporary period is still evolving, and the changes and experiments of the period are ongoing.

Contemporary Pop Styles

Listed below are some American styles that have emerged during the twentieth century. Some of them are still thriving, and new ones are being created every day.

- *Ragtime*—an early style of jazz, very rhythmic and syncopated.
- *Musical Stage Music*—centered around Broadway and Hollywood musicals.
- *Blues*—simple, harmonious melodies with two phrases the same, then one different.
- *Spiritual*—songs originating in the slave culture, usually religious in theme.
- *Jazz*—strong but rhythmic understructure supporting solo and ensemble improvisation.
- *Rock*—strong, steady beat.
- *Country*—based on the folk style of the southern rural United States or on the music of the cowboy.

U.S. satellite put into orbit   U.S. astronaut John Glenn orbits the earth   Voting age lowered from 21 to 18

▼ **1958**   ▼ **1962**   ▼ **1971**

● ●

▲ **1957**   ▲ **1961**   ▲ **1969**

First Earth satellite put into orbit   Soviet cosmonaut orbits the Earth   U.S. astronauts land on the Moon
by USSR

- *Folk*—folk songs and composed songs that tell a story or sometimes have a social message.
- *Reggae*—a fusion of rock and Jamaican rhythms, instruments, and language.
- *Calypso*—an island style with strong chords and syncopation.
- *Tejano*—a fusion of Mexican and country music.
- *Zydeco*—a fusion of African-American, Cajun, and French Canadian rhythms, instruments, and lyrics.

Characteristics of Choral Music During the Contemporary Period

The Contemporary period does not have a characteristic style of music. Still, it is possible to consider major trends in the meter and stress, tempo, dynamics, texture, expressive aspects, and tone quality of Contemporary choral music.

In many Contemporary choral works, meter and stress are an important area of experimentation. A strong rhythmic drive is part of many modern choral works, and unusual changes in meter are often used. The influence of jazz can be heard in the rhythms of many Contemporary choral compositions.

Composers have also experimented with the tempo of their works. The use of various tempos to emphasize changes in mood is common. Dramatic pauses are also used by some composers to heighten the effect of changes in tempo and mood.

The dynamics of most Contemporary choral works reflect an increased use of extremes. Rapid changes and strong accents are often used.

The texture of many Contemporary choral works is developed through dissonance and different methods of resolution. Again, there is much variety in the texture of Contemporary choral music.

The expressive aspects of modern choral works also show unusual variety. In some works, objectivity is very important; in others, personal emotions are dramatically expressed.

The tone quality of Contemporary choral works is typically not extreme. Vibrato is used infrequently and usually with restraint. The skills, control, and exact tuning so important in Renaissance music is again a major feature in the successful performance of Contemporary choral works.

Little League accepts girls

1975

Fall of the Berlin Wall

1989

1972

Robert Moog patents the
Moog synthesizer

1975

U.S. withdraws from Vietnam

1976

U.S. celebrates its 200th birthday

1991

Dissolution of the Union
of Soviet Socialist Republics

Check Your Understanding

Recall

1. What technological developments have affected public involvement in music during the Contemporary period?

2. What is Impressionism?

3. What is abstract music?

4. What is dissonance?

5. Identify two choices that a performer of aleatoric music might be required to make.

6. What is fusion?

7. What style of music has influenced the rhythm of many Contemporary choral works?

8. What tone quality is typically used in Contemporary choral works?

Thinking It Through

1. Eventually, what we call the Contemporary period will be given a new name that reflects the most important trends and developments of the era. What name do you think it will be given? Why?

2. "The more things change, the more they stay the same." What relevance, if any, do you think this statement has for the development of music during the Contemporary period? Explain and defend your opinion.

Listening to . . .
Contemporary Music

CHORAL SELECTION

Stravinsky — *Symphony of Psalms,* First Movement

Igor Stravinsky (1882–1971), a Russian composer, was a leader of contemporary music for over 50 years. His *Symphony of Psalms* (1930) is a masterpiece for chorus and an orchestra with no violins, violas, or clarinets, but including two pianos. It is chantlike in its melodies. He used power as well as humor to produce diversity in his work.

INSTRUMENTAL SELECTION

Stravinsky — "Sacrificial Dance" from *Le Sacre du printemps*

In 1912, the director of the Russian ballet, Sergei Diaghilev, commissioned Stravinsky to write for his troupe. *The Rite of Spring* was a story of a solemn pagan rite: wise elders, seated in a circle, watching a young girl dance herself to death as a sacrifice to the god of spring. At its premiere in 1913, a riot erupted because the audience was so shocked by the pagan primitivism of the dancing and the harsh dissonance and pounding rhythms of the music.

Introducing...
"I Hear America Singing"

André J. Thomas

Setting the Stage

You will enjoy singing "I Hear America Singing" because of its positive text and lively syncopated rhythms. It shows the freedom of contemporary composers who have taken the older form (the spiritual) and reshaped it to fit modern thought. The spiritual expressed the hope of the slaves for release from oppression. Similarly, this piece expresses the hope that America will someday be freed from the oppressions of racism and bigotry and be able to "sing together. . . ," "walk together. . . ," and "shout together. . . ," as one nation and one people.

Meeting the Composer
André J. Thomas

Dr. André J. Thomas is currently Director of Choral Activities and Associate Professor of Music Education at Florida State University in Tallahassee, Florida. Previously, he was on the faculty at the University of Texas in Austin, Texas. In addition to composing and arranging music, he is constantly in demand as an adjudicator, clinician, and director of honor choirs.

I Hear America Singing

Quoting the Spiritual "Walk Together, Children"
COMPOSER: André J. Thomas

CHORAL MUSIC TERMS

accurate pitches

exuberant style

spiritual

syncopated rhythms

VOICING

SATB

PERFORMANCE STYLE

Exuberantly
Accompanied by piano

FOCUS

- Identify and perform syncopated rhythms.
- Sing pitches accurately.
- Sing in exuberant spiritual style.

Warming Up

Vocal Warm-Up

Sing this exercise first on *yo-ho-ho*. Keep the jaw lowered when forming the *y* and form *ee* with your tongue, making the *y* sound free of excess motion.

Now add body movement. Begin with both fists up in front of your shoulders. Extend the fists straight up on beat 1, down on beat 2, and continue alternating through the exercise. Add marching in place after you have mastered the arm motion. Check yourself for pitch accuracy.

Yo - ho-ho, yo - ho-ho, yo - ho-ho, yo - ho-ho, yo - ho-ho, yo - ho-ho, yo - ho-ho, yo.

Yo - ho-ho, yo - ho-ho, yo - ho-ho, yo - ho-ho, yo - ho-ho, yo - ho-ho, yo - ho-ho, yo.

Sight-Singing

Sight-sing this exercise using solfège and hand signs or numbers. You can sing the parts separately or in combination. Rotate the parts, so everyone has a chance to sing the syncopations in Part I against the straighter rhythm of the harmony parts. Tune your pitches accurately.

Sing this exercise in an exuberant, spiritual style. How is this different than just reading the notes?

Singing: "I Hear America Singing"

Music from Africa has made a great impact on music around the world. One of the early forms of African-American music was the spiritual. Combining rhythms and melodic elements of African music with the English language, the early slaves used songs to keep their spirits up. These songs have become symbols of the struggle for equality that still continues around the world.

Find the spirit of "I Hear America Singing" in the combination of old and new, rhythm and melody, music and text. Let that spirit guide your singing style.

Now turn to the music for "I Hear America Singing" on page 220.

HOW DID YOU DO?

Music has the power to communicate the message of a people. Think about your preparation and performance of "I Hear America Singing."

1. How are syncopated rhythms important to this piece? Sing Part I of the Sight-Singing exercise to demonstrate your ability to sing syncopated rhythms.

2. Even when you sing in exuberant style, the pitches must be accurate. Choose a section of "I Hear America Singing" that you can perform in tune, and demonstrate your ability. Choose the most difficult part you can sing accurately.

3. How is exuberant spiritual style different from plain singing? What do you need to do the same, and what is different? Demonstrate with a small group by singing first without this style, then with it.

4. Describe your feelings when you perform "I Hear America Singing" then tell, as best you can, what makes you feel that way.

Dedicated to the 1993 ACDA Honor Choir, Anton Armstrong, Conductor

I Hear America Singing

Quoting the Spiritual "Walk Together, Children"

André J. Thomas

A. J. T. and Trad., alt.

Also available: Special TRAK-PAK 15 (99/1009)

Duration: approx. 2:45.

Don't you __ get wea ry. There's a great camp meet - ing in the

Prom-ised Land. __

Sing to-geth - er, chil - dren.

Don't you __ get wea - ry.

Sing to-geth - er, chil - dren.

Additional Performance Selections

VOICING

SATB

PERFORMANCE STYLE

Mystical
A cappella

Over the Rainbow

Warming Up

Vocal Warm-Up

Practice the octave leaps in this exercise, striving to keep a smooth and connected style. Move up by half steps on the repeat.

Now turn to page **236.**

VOICING

SSAA

PERFORMANCE STYLE

Slowly
Accompanied by piano

Three Canticles for Treble Voices

Warming Up

Vocal Warm-Up

Sing this exercise using solfège and hand signs or numbers. Move up and down by half steps on the repeats. This exercise will increase your ability to sing ascending and descending intervals of a third in sequence.

Now turn to page **241.**

VOICING

TTBB

PERFORMANCE STYLE

With awe
Accompanied by keyboard

Who Is He in Yonder Stall?

Warming Up

Vocal Warm-Up

Sing this exercise using solfège and hand signs or numbers, then with the text. Move up or down by half steps on the repeats. This broken-chord exercise will prepare you to sing the melody of "Who Is He in Yonder Stall?" Use good diaphragmatic action on the eighth notes.

Who ___ is ___ he?   Who ___ is ___ he?

Now turn to page **248.**

VOICING

SATB

PERFORMANCE STYLE

Swing
Accompanied by piano

42nd Street

Warming Up

Vocal Warm-Up

Sing this exercise on *doot*, keeping your energy throughout. Notice the accents on the up-beats, and minor mode. Move up by whole steps on each repeat. The accented upbeats and minor mode will get you in the mood for "42nd Street."

Doot doot

Now turn to page **254.**

VOICING

SATB

PERFORMANCE STYLE

Upbeat swing
Accompanied by guitar, bass,
   drums, and B♭ trumpet

Blue Moon

Warming Up

Vocal Warm-Up

Sing this exercise first using solfège and hand signs or numbers, then on *doo, vah, boh, meh, nee,* or a combination of these syllables. Articulate the rhythms with impeccable precision. Move up or down by half steps on each repeat.

Now turn to page **265.**

VOICING

SSA

PERFORMANCE STYLE

Tranquilly
A cappella

Desde el Fondo de Mi Alma

Warming Up

Vocal Warm-Up

Sing this exercise first using solfège and hand signs or numbers, then on *loo* with legato articulation. Move up by half steps on each repeat. The tranquil, connected style and altered tone will get you ready for "Desde el Fondo de Mi Alma."

Loo loo loo loo ____ loo loo loo.

Now turn to page **273.**

VOICING
SATB

PERFORMANCE STYLE
Slow swing
Accompanied by piano with
optional bass, drums, and guitar

Georgia on My Mind

Warming Up

Vocal Warm-Up
Sing this exercise in jazz style. Swing the eighth notes into triple feel. Change the scat syllables at will—be creative. Move up or down by half steps on the repeat.

Doo-bee doo-bee___ doo-bee.___   Doo-bee doo-bee___ doo-bee.___

Now turn to page **276.**

VOICING
SATB

PERFORMANCE STYLE
Tenderly
Accompanied by piano

Love Never Ends

Warming Up

Vocal Warm-Up
Sing this exercise first on solfège and hand signs or numbers, then with text, continuing up by half steps on the repeats. Notice the octave leap in preparation for "Love Never Ends." Sing with full, deep breaths and confidence to produce a rich, supported, legato sound.

My love ne - ver ends.

Now turn to page **283.**

Over the Rainbow

Music by Harold Arlen
Lyrics by E.Y. Harburg
Arranged by Kirby Shaw

Three Canticles for Treble Voices

1. Tune Me, O Lord

Paul Liljestrand
Christina Rossetti

2. The Master's Touch

Paul Liljestrand
Horatius Bonar

In the still air the music lies un-heard, In the rough marble, beau-ty lies un-seen,

Spare not the stroke, Do with me as Thou wilt.

Let there be nought un - fin - ished, bro - ken,

marred.

Com - plete, O Lord, Thy

marred.

Com - plete Thy

3. The Mirror

Paul Liljestrand
Blanche Mary Kelly

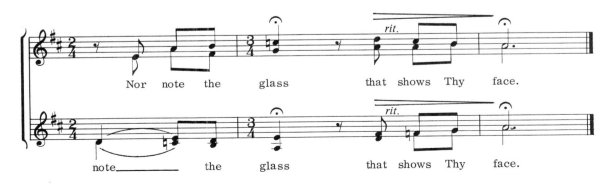

For Wesley Gilliland and the Baylor University Men's Glee Club

Who Is He in Yonder Stall?

Based on "Hanby"

Music by Robert H. Young
Text by Benjamine Hanby

TTBB with Keyboard Accompaniment

* No breath

He _____ in Cal-vary's throes, asks for bless - ings on His

foes? 'Tis the Lord, O won-drous sto - ry, 'tis the

Lord, the King of glo - ry. At His feet we hum - bly

feet we

fall; Crown him, crown Him Lord _____ of _____ all!

crown Him

42nd Street

Music by Harry Warren
Words by Al Dubin
Arranged by Mark Brymer

SATB* and Piano with Optional
Instrumental Accompaniment

*Available for SATB, SAB and SSA
Instrumental Pak includes Parts for
Trumpet I & II, Tenor Sax/Clarinet,
Trombone, Synthesizer, Guitar, Bass
and Drums. ShowTrax Cassette also
available

it's the song I love the mel-o-dy of ___

Dm/F　A7/E　Dm　C/E　F　Gm　Dm/A　B♭9

Unis.

For-ty　Sec-ond _____　Street. _____

Bm7♭5/A　A7♭9♯5　Dm　Em7♭5　Dm/F　A7♯9/E

45

Unis.

Lit-tle "nif-ties"　from the　Fif-ties,　in-no-cent and ___

B♭9

* Performance note: Add additional measures for an optional tap dance break.

gaud - y, _____   *Sport - y _____   For - ty   Sec - ond _____

G/B   C#m7♭5/B   Em7/B   B7♭9#5

Street!

Em   N.C.

8vb _ _ _ _ _ _ _ _ _ _ _ _ _

Unis.   For - ty   Sec - ond   Street!

Unis.   Em/B

8vb _ _ _ _ _ _ _ _ _ _ _ _ _

*pronounced spăwdy

Blue Moon

Music by Richard Rodgers
Lyrics by Lorenz Hart
Arranged by Ruth Artman

SATB, Accompanied with Optional Guitar,
Bass, Drums and B♭ trumpet

*Brushes on snare. L.H. swirl clockwise. R.H. play on beats 2 and 4.

with-out a dream in my heart, ___

with-out a love of my own, ___ *Oo* _____ Blue _ Moon, _

You knew just what I was there ___ for; _

Blue Moon, _____ You knew I was the one for

*Guitar   Eb maj7   Fm7   Eb maj7   Cm7

mf

Cyms. *ad lib.*

*Guitar: Use chord symbols above piano part.

*Solo may be either trumpet or vocal, either as written or ad lib. Vocalist should ad lib. scat syllables.

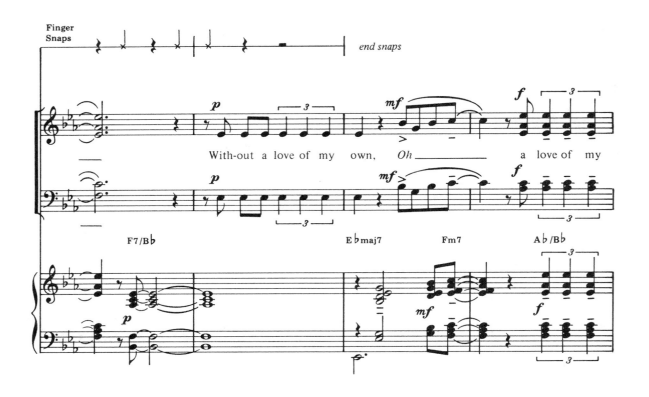

With-out a love of my own, *Oh* ___ a love of my

own! Blue Moon. ___

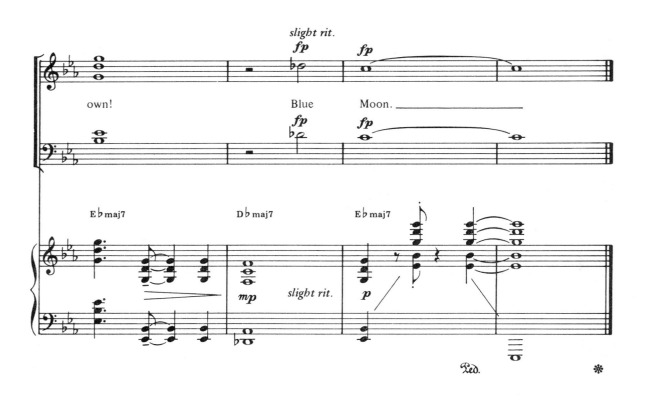

Desde el Fondo de Mi Alma

"Deep Within My Soul's Recesses" (Folk Song)

Music by Domingo Santa Cruz, Op.27
Words Anonymous
English translation by Hugh Ross

SSA with Piano Accompaniment

Georgia on My Mind

Music by Hoagy Carmichael
Lyrics by Stuart Gorrell
Arranged by Teena Chinn

SATB, Accompanied, with Optional Bass,
Drums and Guitar

keeps Geor-gia on my mind, _____

E7   A7   A#dim7 A/B

H.H. Cr.
S.D.

sub. **P**   **ff** *Sop. div.* *rit.* * Slow fall

keeps Geor-gia on my mind. Oh yeah! _____ * Slow fall

sub. **P**

rit.

fill ⌐ ⌐ fill ⌐ ⌐   choke

rit.

* Start fall on second sixteenth after beat 4.

For my sister Barbara on the occasion of her wedding

Love Never Ends

Elizabeth Volk
Adapted from I Corinthians 13

bears all things, be - lieves all things, hopes all things, en -

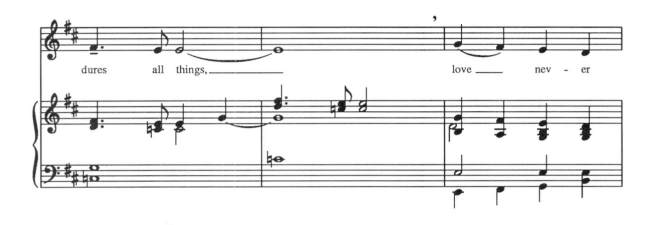

dures all things, _____ love _____ nev - er

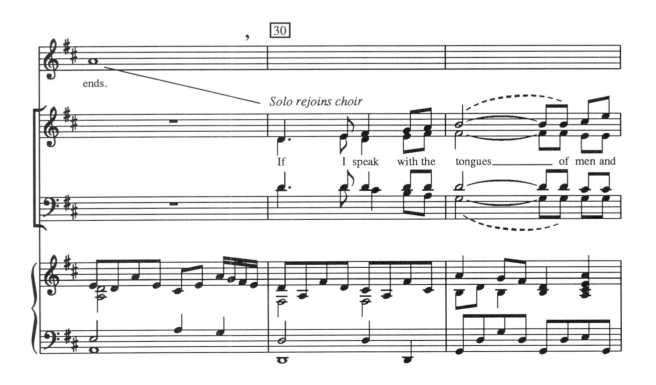

ends.

Solo rejoins choir

If I speak with the tongues _____ of men and

bears all things, be-lieves all things, hopes all things, en-

dures all things, _____ love nev-er ends. _____

Faith, hope, love. _____

Glossary